MTTC 10 Political Science
Teacher Certification Exam

By: Sharon Wynne, M.S
Southern Connecticut State University

"And, while there's no reason yet to panic, I think it's only prudent that we make preparations to panic."

XAMonline, INC.
Boston

To obtain permission(s) to use the material from this work for any purpose including workshops or seminars, please submit a written request to:

XAMonline, Inc.
21 Orient Ave.
Melrose, MA 02176
Toll Free 1-800-301-4647
Email: info@xamonline.com
Web www.xamonline.com
Fax: 1-781-662-9268

Library of Congress Cataloging-in-Publication Data

Wynne, Sharon A.
   Political Science 10: Teacher Certification / Sharon A. Wynne. -2nd ed.
   ISBN 978-1-58197-952-7
   1. Political Science 10.   2. Study Guides.   3. MTTC
   4. Teachers' Certification & Licensure.   5. Careers

Disclaimer:

The opinions expressed in this publication are the sole works of XAMonline and were created independently from the National Education Association, Educational Testing Service, or any State Department of Education, National Evaluation Systems or other testing affiliates.

Between the time of publication and printing, state specific standards as well as testing formats and website information may change that is not included in part or in whole within this product. Sample test questions are developed by XAMonline and reflect similar content as on real tests; however, they are not former tests. XAMonline assembles content that aligns with state standards but makes no claims nor guarantees teacher candidates a passing score. Numerical scores are determined by testing companies such as NES or ETS and then are compared with individual state standards. A passing score varies from state to state.

Printed in the United States of America

MTTC: Political Science 10
ISBN: 978-1-58197-952-7

TABLE OF CONTENTS

Competencies/Skills   **Page Numbers**

Competency 1.0   Political science specialized terminology

Skill 1.1   The vocabulary for American government

Amendment - An amendment is a change or addition to the United States Constitution. Two-thirds of both houses of Congress must propose and then pass one. Or two-thirds of the state legislatures must call a convention to propose one and then it must be ratified by three-fourths of the state legislatures. To date there are only 26 amendments to the Constitution that have passed. An amendment may be used to cancel out a previous one such as the 18th Amendment (1919) known as Prohibition, being canceled by the 21st Amendment (1933).

Articles of Confederation - The first American document that attempted to unite the newly independent colonies after the Revolution. It proved to be unworkable. It was superseded by the Constitution in 1787.

Australian Ballot - A device originated in Australia for choosing candidates for public office. Distinct features include that it is prepared and handled by public officials, paid for with public funds, is secret, and uniform in color and composition. It was used in the United States before the introduction of voting machines in 1892.

Bill Of Rights - The first ten amendments to the United States Constitution dealing with civil liberties and civil rights. They were written mostly by James Madison. They are in brief:

1. **Freedom of Religion.**
2. **Right To Bear Arms.**
3. **Security from the quartering of troops in homes.**
4. **Right against unreasonable search and seizures.**
5. **Right against self-incrimination.**
6. **Right to trial by jury, right to legal council.**
7. **Right to jury trial for civil actions.**
8. **No cruel or unusual punishment allowed.**
9. **These rights shall not deny other rights the people enjoy.**
10. **Powers not mentioned in the Constitution shall be retained by the states or the people.**

Checks and Balances - System set up by the Constitution in which each branch of the federal government has the power to check, or limit the actions of other branches.

Confederate States of America - The nation formed by the states that seceded from the federal Union around 1860 and 1861. It ceased to exist after its loss in the American Civil War in 1865.

Congress - In the United States it is the supreme legislative assembly. It is a bicameral body, (one that consists of two parts), the **House of Representatives** and the **Senate**.

Constitution - The written document that describes and defines the system and structure of the United States government. Ratification of the Constitution by the required number of states, (nine of the original thirteen), was completed on June 21, *1788,* and thus the Constitution officially became the law of the land.

Constitutional Convention - Meeting of delegates from 12 states who wrote a new constitution for the United States in 1787.

County - A unit of local government formerly known in Great Britain as "shire." All states now have county governments except for Louisiana, (which prefers the term "parish"), Alaska, and Connecticut.

Declaration Of Independence - The document that stated that the British colonies in America had become a free and independent nation, adopted July 4, 1776.

Democracy - A form of government in which the people rule. The word "democrat" comes from the ancient Greek "demo"-people and "kratia"-to rule.

Democracy (Direct) - A form of government in which the people assemble at a specific period and times to perform the functions usually delegated to a representative legislature. Sometimes the term "pure" democracy is used. It was prevalent in ancient Greece.

Democracy (Indirect) - A form of government in which the people rule through elected representatives in a legislature. Sometimes called a **"republican"** form of government, or **"democracy in republic,"** the United States is this form of government.

Executive - A branch of the federal government. It consists of two office-holders, a President and a Vice-President, elected by indirect election for a period of four years. The President is responsible for carrying out the laws of Congress. The President may also propose new laws for Congressional consideration. (See: President and Vice-President)

Federal - It is the organization of the government of the United States. It consists of two parts that are the national government based in Washington DC and the various individual state governments.

House of Representatives - It is part of the bicameral legislature of the United States chosen by direct election based on population for a period of two years. An individual must be twenty-five years old and a citizen of the United States for seven years in order to be eligible to be elected.

Legislative - The law making branch of the government. In the United States, it is bicameral, consisting of the House of Representatives and the Senate.

Magna Carta - The document that guaranteed rights to English nobles, forced on the British King John in 1215. It is considered an important forerunner to the idea of government having a written limitation of its power.

Manifest Destiny - Belief of many Americans in the 1840s that the United States should own all the land between the Atlantic and Pacific oceans.

Monroe Doctrine - Policy statement made by President James Monroe in 1823 that warned the European powers that the United States considered the American continent and the western hemisphere as its special sphere of influence and that others should stay out of it.

Pocket Veto - When a President neither signs or "officially" has vetoed a bill. If within ten days, (not including Sundays), Congress adjourns the bill is killed. If Congress is in session, the bill will automatically become a law. (See: Veto)

Popular Sovereignty - In American history in the 19th century, right of territorial inhabitants applying for statehood to determine whether or not their state would or would not permit slavery.

President - The Chief Executive of the United States, responsible for carrying out the laws passed by Congress, Commander In Chief of the armed forces, elected by indirect election for a period of four years. One must have been born a citizen and thirty-five years old in order to be eligible to be elected. (See: Executive)

Primary Election - Election in which candidates from a particular political party are chosen to run for office. As a rule, usually, only registered party members are allowed to vote in such elections.

Representative Government - Type of government in which voters elect representatives to make laws for them. (See: indirect democracy)

Senate - Part of the bicameral legislature of the United States government, consisting of two members from each state (one hundred members at present) chosen by direct election for a period of six years. An individual must be thirty years old and a citizen of the United States for nine years in order to be eligible to be elected.

Separation of Powers - System of American government in which each branch of government has its own specifically designated powers and can not interfere with the powers of another.

States' Rights - Idea that the individual states had the right to limit the power of the federal government, that the states' authority should be supreme within it, as opposed to guidance from the federal government. An important contributing factor in the American Civil War.

Supreme Court - It is the highest court in the land and the court of final appeal. Only court of law specifically established by the Constitution.

Unitary Government - A form of government in which power is held by the central government which may or may not choose to delegate power to lesser governmental units. Examples are Great Britain, France and Israel. As opposed to *"Federal Government",* in which power is shared by national and state governments. (See: Federal)

Veto - To oppose a motion or enactment of a law from taking effect.

Vice-President - Assistant to the President, his immediate successor in case of disability or death. He also functions as the President of the Senate when it is in session. (See: Executive)

Skill 1.2 The vocabulary for law studies.

Bail - Money left with the court in order for an individual to be released from jail pending trial. When an individual returns for trial the money is returned. If one flees the money is forfeited.

Civil - A lawsuit brought before a court usually to recover monetary funds as opposed to a criminal action brought for a penal offense.

Criminal - A penal crime, one that normally results in an imposition of a term of imprisonment, or of a monetary fine by the state or both.

Double Jeopardy - Subjecting an accused person to repeated trials for the same criminal offense. Forbidden by the Fifth Amendment to the Constitution.

Due Process - The right of a defendant to go through the established legal system before imprisonment i.e. trial, have legal counsel, verdict rendered in a court of law.

Equity - A branch of civil law that provides remedial justice when there is no remedy in common or prescribed law.

Grand Jury - As specified in the Constitution, it is a body of persons called to hear complaints of the commission of criminal offenses and to determine if enough evidence is available for a criminal indictment. It is normally composed of twelve to twenty-four individuals who hear the evidence and deliberate in private.

Habeas Corpus - The right to appear in court in order to determine if an imprisonment is lawful. Also known as a *"Writ of Habeas Corpus."*

Exclusionary Rule - As defined from the Fourth and Fifth Amendments, it is the inability of evidence seized unlawfully or statements gathered wrongly, to be brought into a court of law.

Ex Post Facto Law - A law created to punish an act after it has been committed. Prohibited by the Constitution, i.e. you can not prosecute someone for an act, if it was legal at the time, although a law was subsequently enacted against it.

Impeach - To bring charges against an official in the government such as the President. In the case of the President, the House of Representatives is the only branch of government empowered to bring such charges. They are then tried in the Senate.

Judicial Review - The right of the court to review laws and acts of the legislature and executive branches and to declare them unconstitutional. (Established in *"Marbury* vs. *Madison"* 1803).

Judiciary - The legal system, including but not limited to, courts of law and appeal.

Judiciary Act - Law that organized the federal court system into Federal and Circuit Courts in 1789.

Jurisprudence - Of relating to, or pertaining to, the law or the legal system and its practice or exercise thereof.

Miranda Warning - As defined from the Fifth and Sixth Amendments. The right to remain silent so one does not incriminate oneself and the right to legal counsel during questioning.

Penal - Having to do with punishment, most often in regards to imprisonment and incarceration by the state.

Tort - A private or civil action brought before a court of law i.e. a civil lawsuit.

Skill 1.3   The vocabulary for international relations.

Balance of Trade - The difference between the value of goods a given nation exports and the value of goods it imports.

Boycott - The refusal to buy certain goods or services of one party from another based on a specific grievance.

Embargo - The ban on trade between one country and another based on a conflict that exists between them.

European Union - An economic and political organization of European countries that allows free trade among the member countries.

General Agreement On Tariffs and Trade (GATT) - The periodic international conference that meets to reduce trade barriers among member countries.

Group of Seven - Group of nations that meet to promote negotiations and coordinate economic relations and agreements among the member countries. The seven are: The *United States, Japan, Germany, Great Britain, France, Canada, and Italy.* (The "Group of Five" excludes Canada and Italy).

International - Having to do with more than one nation, relationships between nations.

International Law - System of legal statutes set up and agreed upon by several individual nations regulating conduct between them. The International Court of Law as established in the United Nations charter is located in The Hague, in The Netherlands.

International Monetary Fund - A multinational institution concerned mostly with world financial issues.

Nation - The modern establishment of a political community covering a set geographic area, population, and laws. Evolved from the primitive city-state of ancient times.

Nationalism - Strong pride in one's own country, sometimes taken to an extreme and in believing that one's own country is superior to all others, can be an important cause of war.

Parliamentary System - A system of government with a legislature, usually involving a multiplicity of political parties and often coalition politics. There is division between the head of state and head of government. Head of government is usually known as a Prime Minister who is also usually the head of the largest party. The head of government and cabinet usually both sit and vote in the parliament. Head of state is most often an elected president, (though in the case of a constitutional monarchy, like Great Britain, the sovereign may take the place of a president as head of state). A government may fall when a majority in parliament votes "no confidence" in the government.

Presidential System - A system of government with a legislature, can involve few or many political parties, no division between head of state and head of government. The President serves in both capacities. The President is elected either by direct or indirect election. A President and cabinet usually do not sit or vote in the legislature and The President may or may not be the head of the largest political party. A President can thus rule even without a majority in the legislature. He can only be removed from office before an election for major infractions of the law.

State - A political community covering a set geographic area, population and laws. Can be another name for nation.

Tariff - The tax that a government places on internationally traded goods, most often imported goods.

Treaty - A document between individual nation-states covering specific areas of agreement.

United Nations - International organization established in 1945 at the close of the Second World War. It replaced the defunct League of Nations. World headquarters is located in **New York City,** though various agencies are located in several different world cities, such as the World Court in The Hague, in The Netherlands.

World Bank - International institution set up to assist developing nations by helping them to secure low interest loans.

World Court - International body based in The Netherlands city of **The Hague** that was established by the original United Nations Charter. Set up to peacefully mediate disputes among the member nations and to investigate violations of agreed international law.

Skill 1.4   Other major political systems

Anarchism - Political movement believing in the elimination of all government and its replacement by a cooperative community of individuals. Sometimes it has involved political violence such as assassinations of important political or governmental figures. The historical banner of the movement is a black flag.

Communism - A belief as well as a political system, characterized by the ideology of class conflict and revolution, one party state and dictatorship, repressive police apparatus, and government ownership of the means of production and distribution of goods and services. A revolutionary ideology preaching the eventual overthrow of all other political orders and the establishment of one world Communist government.   Same as Marxism. The historical banner of the movement is a red flag and variation of stars, hammer and sickles, representing the various types of workers. (See **Karl Marx** Section 5.3, **Communism** Section 5.4).

Dictatorship - The rule by an individual or small group of individuals (Oligarchy) that centralizes all political control in itself and enforces its will with a terrorist police force.

Fascism - A belief as well as a political system, opposed ideologically to Communism, though similar in basic structure, with a one party state, centralized political control and a repressive police system. It however tolerates private ownership of the means of production, though it maintains tight overall control. Central to its belief is the idolization of the Leader, a "Cult of the Personality," and most often an expansionist ideology. Examples have been German Nazism and Italian Fascism. (See: Fascism, Section 5.4)

Monarchy - The rule of a nation by a Monarch, (a non-elected usually hereditary leader), most often a king, or queen. It may or may not be accompanied by some measure of democracy open institutions and elections at various levels. A modern example is Great Britain, where it is called a Constitutional Monarchy.

Socialism - Political belief and system in which the state takes a guiding role in the national economy and provides extensive social services to its population. It may or may not own outright means of production, but even where it does not, it exercises tight control. It usually promotes democracy, (Democratic Socialism), though the heavy state involvement produces excessive bureaucracy and usually inefficiency. Taken to an extreme it may lead to Communism as government control increases and democratic practice decrease. Ideologically the two movements are very similar in both belief and practice, as Socialists also preach the superiority of their system to all others and that it will become the eventual natural order. It is also considered for that reason a variant of Marxism. It also has used a red flag as a symbol. (See Karl Marx, Section 5.3)

Competency 2.0   Methods of presenting diagrammatic information

Skill 2.1   Understanding illustrations, (maps, graphs, and charts)

We use **illustrations** of various sorts because it is often easier to demonstrate a given idea visually instead of orally. Sometimes it is even easier to do so with an illustration than a description. This is especially true in the areas of education and research because humans are visually stimulated. It is a fact that any idea presented visually in some manner is always easier to understand and to comprehend than simply getting an idea across verbally, by hearing it or reading it. Throughout this document, there are several illustrations that have been presented to explain an idea in a more precise way. Sometimes these will demonstrate some of the types of illustrations available for use in the arena of political science. Among the more common illustrations used in political science are various types of **maps, graphs and charts**.

Photographs and globes are useful as well, but as they are limited in what kind of information that they can show, they are rarely used. Unless, as in the case of a photograph, it is of a particular political figure or a time that one wishes to visualize.

Although maps have advantages over globes and photographs, they do have a major disadvantage. This problem must be considered as well. The major problem of all maps comes about because most maps are flat and the Earth is a sphere. It is impossible to reproduce exactly on a flat surface an object shaped like a sphere. In order to put the earth's features onto a map they must be stretched in some way. This stretching is called **distortion.**

Distortion does not mean that maps are wrong, it simply means that they are not perfect representations of the Earth or its parts. **Cartographers,** or mapmakers, understand the problems of distortion. They try to design them so that there is as little distortion as possible in the maps.

The process of putting the features of the Earth onto a flat surface is called **projection**. All maps are really map projections. There are many different types. Each one deals in a different way with the problem of distortion. Map projections are made in a number of ways. Some are done using complicated mathematics. However, the basic ideas behind map projections can be understood by looking at the three most common types:

(1) **Cylindrical Projections** - These are done by taking a cylinder of paper and wrapping it around a globe. A light is used to project the globe's features onto the paper. Distortion is least where the paper touches the globe. For example, suppose that the paper was wrapped so that it touched the globe at the equator, the map from this projection would have just a little distortion near the equator.

However, in moving north or south of the equator, the distortion would increase as you moved further away from the equator. The best known and most widely used cylindrical projection is the **Mercator Projection.** It was first developed in 1569 by Gerardus Mercator, a Flemish mapmaker.

(2). **Conical Projections** - The name for these maps come from the fact that the projection is made onto a cone of paper. The cone is made so that it touches a globe at the base of the cone only. It can also be made so that it cuts through part of the globe in two different places. Again, there is the least distortion where the paper touches the globe. If the cone touches at two different points, there is some distortion at both of them. Conical projections are most often used to map areas in the **middle latitudes**. Maps of the United States are most often conical projections. This is because most of the country lies within these latitudes.

(3). **Flat-Plane Projections** - These are made with a flat piece of paper. It touches the globe at one point only. Areas near this point show little distortion. Flat-plane projections are often used to show the areas of the north and south poles. One such flat projection is called a **Gnomonic Projection**. On this kind of map all meridians appear as straight lines, Gnomonic projections are useful because any straight line drawn between points on it forms a **Great-Circle Route**. Great-Circle Routes can best be described by thinking of a globe and when using the globe the shortest route between two points on it can be found by simply stretching a string from one point to the other. However, if the string was extended in reality, so that it took into effect the globe's curvature, it would then make a great-circle. A great-circle is any circle that cuts a sphere, such as the globe, into two equal parts. Because of distortion, most maps do not show great-circle routes as straight lines, Gnomonic projections, however, do show the shortest distance between the two places as a straight line, because of this they are valuable for navigation. They are called Great-Circle Sailing Maps.

To properly analyze a given map one must be familiar with the various parts and symbols that most modern maps use. For the most part, this is standardized, with different maps using similar parts and symbols, these can include:

The Title - All maps should have a title, just like all books should. The title tells you what information is to be found on the map.

The Legend - Most maps have a legend. A legend tells the reader about the various symbols that are used on that particular map and what the symbols represent, (also called a *map key)*.

The Grid - A grid is a series of lines that are used to find exact places and locations on the map. There are several different kinds of grid systems in use, however, most maps do use the longitude and latitude system, known as the **Geographic Grid System**.

Directions - Most maps have some directional system to show which way the map is being presented. Often on a map, a small compass will be present, with arrows showing the four basic directions, north, south, east, and west.

The Scale - This is used to show the relationship between a unit of measurement on the map versus the real world measure on the Earth. Maps are drawn to many different scales. Some maps show a lot of detail for a small area. Others show a greater span of distance, whichever is being used one should always be aware of just what scale is being used. For instance the scale might be something like 1 inch = 10 miles for a small area or for a map showing the whole world it might have a scale in which 1 inch = 1,000 miles. The point is that one must look at the map key in order to see what units of measurements the map is using.

Maps have four main properties. They are (1) the size of the areas shown on the map. (2) The shapes of the areas, (3) Consistent scales, and (4) Straight line directions. A map can be drawn so that it is correct in one or more of these properties. No map can be correct in all of them.

Equal areas - One property which maps can have is that of equal areas, In an equal area map, the meridians and parallels are drawn so that the areas shown have the same proportions as they do on the Earth. For example, Greenland is about 118th the size of South America, thus it will be show as 118th the size on an equal area map. The **Mercator projection** is an example of a map that does not have equal areas. In it, Greenland appears to be about the same size of South America. This is because the distortion is very bad at the poles and Greenland lies near the North Pole.

Conformality - A second map property is conformality, or correct shapes. There are no maps which can show very large areas of the earth in their exact shapes. Only globes can really do that, however Conformal Maps are as close as possible to true shapes. The United States is often shown by a Lambert Conformal Conic Projection Map.

Consistent Scales - Many maps attempt to use the same scale on all parts of the map. Generally, this is easier when maps show a relatively small part of the earth's surface. Generally maps showing large areas are not consistent-scale maps. This is so because of distortion. Often such maps will have two scales noted in the key. One scale, for example, might be accurate to measure distances between points along the Equator. Another might be then used to measure distances between the North Pole and the South Pole.

Maps showing physical features often try to show information about the elevation or *relief* of the land. *Elevation* is the distance above or below the sea level. The elevation is usually shown with colors, for instance, all areas on a map which are at a certain level will be shown in the same color.

Relief Maps - Show the shape of the land surface, flat, rugged, or steep. Relief maps usually give more detail than simply showing the overall elevation of the land's surface. Relief is also sometimes shown with colors, but another way to show relief is by using *contour lines*. These lines connect all points of a land surface which are the same height surrounding the particular area of land.

Thematic Maps - These are used to show more specific information, often on a single *theme,* or topic. Thematic maps show the distribution or amount of something over a certain given area. Things such as population density, climate, economic information, cultural, political information, etc ...

Political science would be almost impossible without maps. Information can be gained looking at a map that might take hundreds of words to explain otherwise. Maps reflect the great variety of knowledge covered by political science. To show such a variety of information maps are made in many different ways. Because of this variety, maps must be understood in order to make the best sense of them. Once they are understood, maps provide a solid foundation for political science studies.

To apply information obtained from *graphs* one must understand the two major reasons why graphs are used:

1. To present a <u>model or theory</u> *visually in order to show how two or more variables interrelate.*
2. To present <u>real world</u> *data visually in order to show how two or more variables interrelate.*

Most often used are those known as *bar graphs* and *line graphs*. (Charts are often used for similar reasons and are explained in the next section).

Graphs themselves are most useful when one wishes to demonstrate the sequential increase, or decrease of a variable or to show specific correlations between two or more variables in a given circumstance.

Most common is the *bar graph*. Because it has an easy to see and understand way of visually showing the difference in a given set of variables. However it is limited in that it can not really show the actual proportional increase, or decrease, of each given variable to each other. (In order to show a decrease, a bar graph must show the "bar" under the starting line, thus removing the ability to really show how the various different variables would relate to each other).

Thus in order to accomplish this one must use a **line graph**. Line graphs can be of two types a *linear* or *non-linear* graph. A linear line graph uses a series of straight lines, a non-linear line graph uses a curved line. Though the lines can be either straight or curved, all of the lines are called *curves*.

A line graph uses a number line or *axis.* The numbers are generally placed in order, equal distances from one another, the number line is used to represent a number, degree or some such other variable at an appropriate point on the line. Two lines are used, intersecting at a specific point. They are referred to as the X-axis and the Y-axis. The Y-axis is a vertical line the X-axis is a horizontal line. Together they form a *coordinate system.* The difference between a point on the line of the X-axis and the Y-axis is called the *slope* of the line, or the change in the value on the vertical axis divided by the change in the value on the horizontal axis. The Y-axis number is called the *rise* and the X-axis number is called the *run,* thus the equation for slope is:

> *SLOPE* = *RISE* - (*Change in value on the vertical axis*)
> *RUN* - (*Change in value on the horizontal axis*)

The slope tells the amount of increase or decrease of a given *specific* variable. When using two or more variables one can plot the amount of difference between them in any given situation. This makes presenting information on a line graph more involved. It also makes it more informative and accurate than a simple bar graph. Knowledge of the term slope and what it is and how it is measured helps us to describe verbally the pictures we are seeing visually. For example, if a curve is said to have a slope of "zero", you should picture a flat line. If a curve has a slope of "one", you should picture a rising line that makes a 45-degree angle with the horizontal and vertical axis lines.

The preceding examples are of *linear* (straight line) curves. With *non-linear* curves (the ones that really do curve) the slope of the curve is constantly changing, so as a result, we must then understand that the slope of the non-linear curved line will be at *a* specific point. How is this done? The slope of a non-linear curve is determined by the slope of a straight line *that intersects the curve at that specific point.*

In all graphs, an upward sloping line represents a direct relationship between the two variables. A downward slope represents an inverse relationship between the two variables. In reading any graph, one must always be very careful to understand what is being measured, what can be deduced and what cannot be deduced from the given graph.

To use **charts** correctly, one should remember the reasons one uses graphs. The general ideas are similar. It is usually a question as to which, a graph or chart, is more capable of adequately portraying the information one-wants to illustrate. One can see the difference between them and realize that in many ways graphs and charts are interrelated. One of the most common types, because it is easiest to read and understand, even for the lay person, is the **Pie-chart**.

You can see pie-charts used often, especially when one is trying to illustrate the differences in percentages among various items, or when one is demonstrating the divisions of a whole.

Realistically, one can make a chart out of almost any multiple set of variables. Remember to properly show the differences between them, what you are trying to prove and keep it clear enough to read and understand with a minimum of effort. The usefulness of a chart is wasted if too much time is taken in order to understand it. Charts are always used to simplify an idea, NEVER to complicate it.

As stated before, in political science and related fields, all type of illustrations, maps, graphs and charts are useful tools for both education and research. As such, they quite often are used to better demonstrate an idea than simply stating it since there are some problems and situations that are easier to understand visually than verbally. They are also better in trying to show relationships between any given set of variables or circumstances. However one must always remember that though a picture may "be worth a thousand words", it still can't say everything and one should always be aware of the limits of any diagrammatic model. In other words," *seeing is not always, necessarily, believing*".

Competency 3.0   Methods of data gathering

Skill 3.1   **The study of demography, demographic tables, and statistics**

Demography is the branch of science of statistics most concerned with the social well being of people. **Demographic tables** may include: (1) Analysis of the population on the basis of age, parentage, physical condition, race, occupation and civil position, giving the actual size and the density of each separate area. (2) Changes in the population as a result of birth, marriage, and death. (3) Statistics on population movements and their effects and their relations to given economic, social and political conditions. (4) Statistics of crime, illegitimacy and suicide. (5) Levels of education and economic and social statistics.

Such information is also similar to that area of science known as **vital statistics** and as such is indispensable in studying social trends and making important legislative, economic, and social decisions. Such demographic information is gathered from census, and registrar reports and the like, and by state laws such information, especially the vital kind, is kept by physicians, attorneys, funeral directors, member of the clergy, and similar professional people. In the United States such demographic information is compiled, kept and published by the Public Health Service of the United States Department of Health, Education, and Welfare.

The most important element of this information is the so-called **rate**, which customarily represents the average of births and deaths for a unit of 1000 population over a given calendar year. These general rates are called **crude rates**, which are then sub-divided into *sex, color, age, occupation, locality, etc.* They are then known as **refined rates**.

In examining **statistics** and the sources of statistical data one must also be aware of the methods of statistical information gathering. For instance, there are many good sources of raw statistical data. Books such as *The Statistical Abstract of the United States,* published by the United States Chamber of Commerce, *The World Fact Book,* published by the Central Intelligence Agency or *The Monthly Labor Review* published by the United States Department of Labor are excellent examples that contain much raw data. Many such yearbooks and the like on various topics are readily available from any library, or from the government itself. However, knowing how that data and information was gathered is at least equally as important as the figures themselves. Because only by having knowledge of statistical language and methodology, can one really be able to gauge the usefulness of any given piece of data presented. Thus we must first understand just what statistics are and what they can and cannot, tell us.

Simply put, statistics is the mathematical science that deals with the collection, organization, presentation, and analysis of various forms of numerical data and with the problems such as interpreting and understanding such data. The raw materials of statistics are sets of numbers obtained from enumerations or measurements collected by various methods of extrapolation, such as census taking, interviews, and observations.

In collecting any such statistical information and data, care and adequate precautions must always be taken in order to assure that the knowledge obtained is complete and accurate. It is also important to be aware of just how much data is necessary to collect in order to establish the idea that is attempting to be formulated. One important idea to understand is that statistics usually deal with a specific **model**, **hypothesis**, or **theory** that is being attempted to be proven. Though one should be aware that a theory can never actually be proved correct it can only really be corroborated. (**Corroboration** meaning that the data presented is more consistent with this theory than with any other theory, so it makes sense to use this theory.) One should also be aware of what is known as **correlation** (the joint movement of various data points) does not infer **causation** (the change in one of those data points caused the other data points to change). It is important that one take these aspects into account so that one can be in a better position to appreciate what the collected data is really saying

Once collected, data must then be arranged, tabulated, and presented to permit ready and meaningful analysis and interpretation. Often tables, charts or graphs will be used to present the information in a concise easy to see manner, with the information sometimes presented in raw numerical order as well. **Tests of reliability** are used, bearing in mind the manner in which the data has been collected and the inherent biases of any artificially created model to be used to explain real world events. Indeed the methods used and the inherent biases and reasons actually for doing the study by the individual(s) involved, must never be discounted.

So one should always remember that statistical methods can and have been used to prove or disprove historically just about anything. While statistics are a good and important empirical research tool, too much reliance on them alone, without any other information or data, can be misleading and statistics should only be used with other empirical methods of research. As the famous saying goes, *"Figures don't lie, but liars always figure."*

Competency 4.0   Information interpretation skills

Skill 4.1   Differentiating fact from opinion

"The sky is blue", "the sky looks like rain", one a fact and the other an opinion. This is because one is **readily provable by objective empirical data**, while the other is a **subjective evaluation based upon personnel bias**. This means that facts are things that can be proved by the usual means of study and experimentation. We can look and see the color of the sky. Since the shade we are observing is expressed as the color blue and is an accepted norm, the observation that the sky is blue is therefore a fact. (Of course, this depends on other external factors such as time and weather conditions).

This brings us to our next idea, that it looks like rain. This is a subjective observation in that an individual's perception will differ from another. What looks like rain to one person will not necessarily look like that to another.

This is an important concept to understand since much of what actually is studied in political science is, in reality, simply the opinions of various political theorists and philosophers. The truth of their individual philosophies is demonstrated by how well they, (when they have been tried), work in the so called "real world."

The question thus remains as to how to differentiate fact from opinion. The best and only way is to ask oneself if what is being stated can be proved from other sources, by other methods, or by the simple process of **reasoning**.

Skill 4.2   The reliability of media sources

In looking at the reliability of media sources, one must always be aware of the central fact of the human condition in that anything one does will naturally be colored in some way by a person's own personal belief system, biases and ones prejudices. The fact is that objectivity in the real world is really impossible and perhaps may be in reality, also, undesirable. This is because it would then have to imply a virtual and total detachment from reality and concerns. Humans are rational beings, but also humans are emotional beings and this emotionalism must color their perceptions. In fact, we must remember when looking at the media it does concern real life, individuals, and events, usually of a sensational or at least very important nature. One could then expect biases to be that much more, rather than less, pronounced: This is owing to the very nature of the events that are being reported.

In fact, recent surveys done in the major media have found a pronounced personal bias, at least in beliefs. For instance, the surveys have demonstrated that of the major broadcast media 85% have identified themselves either as liberal, or members of the Democratic Party or both.

Now this might be too broad a statement, but the fact remains that many in the media do tend to align themselves with policies or ideas that can be considered left-leaning or "liberal". Many have explained this by saying that a field like the media and investigative journalism would naturally lend itself to those individuals who would be either inquisitive or believe in questioning authority and the accepted norm. To be cynical perhaps in believing what they are told or have been led to believe either in growing up, in school or in the larger society. They thus would be people who would be looking to get to the "real" truth of a matter. Such types would tend to be on the "left" side of politics since that is the side (the "radicals") that has been historically the one to question the "Establishment". To be challenging what is perceived to be "conservative" institutions.

Historically it has also been true that the media, being a for profit enterprise, exists in a contradictory manner in and of itself. For instance, if we accept the fact that the media is composed of individuals who tend to question and inquire of those in authority, then to them, the issue of arriving at the "truth" of an issue would be paramount. They would not allow any monetary or financial issues or considerations to interfere. However, it is also true that by and large, the major media in this country is privately owned and is usually looking for a profit. Thus, these two ideas may or may not become in conflict with each other at different times.

This is owed to the fact that though average journalists may be dedicated to their profession, looking only to arrive at the "real story", the ownership of the major media tends to be corporate and are part of the "Establishment". They may be as dedicated as their employees to the search for "truth and justice". Unlike the journalists who work for them, the ownership must be constantly looking at the "bottom-line".

To put it bluntly, a news organization must make money in order to survive, (at least, again in this country they must. There are some exceptions. For all practical purposes, those media sources who claim to be non-profit or claim to be working in the public good have a limited influence).

So the news media will do what it has to in order to get a story and will try to get it no matter what or who it may offend. They must also be conscious of their prospective audience and must be careful not to turn them off, (lest they themselves get "turned off" or go unread). This type of financial consideration can even lead certain media organizations at specific times to go out of their way to report stories that are best described as "sensationalistic" or "exploitative".

For instance, during the Spanish-American War at the turn of the century, the Hearst newspaper chain took a very favorable view of the war. It was even accused of fomenting a "war fever" in the country based on its reporting. The term *"yellow journalism"* has been coined for instances such as this, in which the media takes what could be considered an extreme or unethical position or one in which not all of the pertinent facts are revealed. Thus, the media is attempting to not only report the news, but rather to influence public opinion. Another form of what has been called extremism in reporting is called *"muckraking"*. This is when the media goes after what it perceives to be unethical or corrupt behavior on the part of public officials. The fact that makes this a derogatory term, (in regards to what many consider to be an important job of the media), is the excessive zeal in which a particular media outlet may be pursuing the story. Thus important facts, or circumstances may be left out, or even totally ignored if a particular point of view is being promoted by the given media source. The media does often play to what is called *sensationalism* for the very reasons previously mentioned.

It is very important to be aware that though the media plays an important role in a country's life, it is still subject to the same failings, biases, and prejudices of other aspects of human society. One must always be aware of this fact in any careful analysis of information gathered by this source. Or as the saying goes *"you can't believe everything you read",* (and see or hear for that matter).

Competency 5.0   Knowledge of government

Skill 5.1   The functions of government.

Historically the functions of government, or people's concepts of government and its purpose and function, have varied considerably. In the theory of political science, the function of government is to secure the common welfare of the members of the given society over which it exercises control. In different historical eras, governments have attempted to achieve the common welfare by various means in accordance with the traditions and ideology of the given society. Among *primitive peoples*, systems of control were rudimentary at best. They arose directly from the ideas of right and wrong that had been established in the group and were common in that particular society. Control being exercised most often by means of group pressure, most often in the forms of taboos and superstitions and in many cases by ostracism, or banishment from the group. Thus, in most cases, because of the extreme tribal nature of society in those early times, this lead to very unpleasant circumstances for the individual so treated. Without the protection of the group, a lone individual was most often in for a sad and very short, fate. (No other group would accept such an individual into their midst and survival alone was extremely difficult if not impossible).

Among more *civilized peoples*, governments began to assume more institutional forms. They rested on a well-defined legal basis. They imposed penalties on violators of the social order. They used force, which was supported and sanctioned by their people. The government was charged to establish the social order and was supposed to do so in order to be able to discharge its functions.

Eventually the ideas of government, who should govern and how, came to be considered by various thinkers and philosophers. The most influential of these and those who had the most influence on our present society were the ancient Greek philosophers such as Plato and Aristotle.

Aristotle's conception of government was based on a simple idea. The function of government was to provide for the general welfare of its people. A good government, and one that should be supported, was one that did so in the best way possible, with the least pressure on the people.   Bad governments were those that subordinated the general welfare to that of the individuals who ruled. At no time should any function of any government be that of personal interest of any one individual, no matter who that individual was. This does not mean that Aristotle had no sympathy for the individual or individual happiness (as at times Plato has been accused by those who read his "***Republic,***" which was the first important philosophical text to explore these issues). Rather Aristotle believed that a society is greater than the sum of its parts, or that "the good of the many outweighs the good of the few and also of the one".

Yet, a good government and one that is carrying out its functions well, will always weigh the relative merits of what is good for a given individual in society and what is good for the society as a whole.

This basic concept has continued to our own time and has found its fullest expression in the idea of representative democracy and political and personal freedom. In addition, a government that maintains good social order, while allowing the greatest possible exercise of autonomy for individuals to achieve.

Skill 5.2 The origin of the "state."

The idea and concept of the "state" or of the organization of people into large political bodies covering a specific area is an old and universal one. Throughout the world all societies at one time or another have gone though various stages of organization that can at times be loosely defined as a "state". Some have continued into advanced stages, others have never passed the most primitive forms and thus can best be described as "tribes", or "clans" and never advancing further.

It is the culture known as "**The West**" i.e. the United States and Western Europe, that have utilized these processes the most and have been most advanced in what they have managed to achieve. Specifically, in forcing their form of government on others. These forms have in any case proven the most enduring. Some would perhaps not consider this necessarily a virtue, or even a desirable situation, but it is a fact and the one in which we must function. It is primarily how this came to be that we would examine.

Most modern theories of the origin of the state tend to agree on several key ideas differing only on the emphasis placed on each succeeding stage and its relative importance or duration. The stages can be identified as such:

In ancient times, early peoples developed primitive weapons and tools but were nomadic and mostly banded together in primitive hunting groups or "clans" in order to maximize their effectiveness in the hunt. The more people that went after the prey the easier it would be to find it and kill it.

In later times, when hunting grew scarce, people still banded together for protection from other clans in order to protect the diminishing available hunting grounds.

Still later, when hunting no longer was able to sustain the clans they gradually turned to *hunting and gathering*. Hunting when feasible, gathering fruits, vegetables, roots and berries and the like when there was no hunting available. These became known as *hunter-gatherer* societies and the first to begin to remain in one place for a time.

However, it was not until the invention of the *plow and* the fact that it made *farming* easier that people began to be able to remain in one place for a long time. With farming, supplying sufficient food to enable the first large organized *city-states* to emerge. This occurred on a large scale first in the ancient Mesopotamian region near the Tigris and Euphrates Rivers in what is now modern Iraq. The first large, organized city-states were those of the land known as *Sumer* or *Sumeria*, later known as the land of Babylonia.

In time, these early primitive city-states began to become united and to form bigger unions for greater protection and power. With each emerging new "nation" or "state" claiming control over a specific area of land and willing to fight for it.

Thus, with the emergence of the first large nations, the first large organized armies also came into being and regular warfare emerged as a universal and historical fact of human existence.

By the time known as the *classical period* of ancient history, that of ancient Egypt, Greece and Rome, the city-state had emerged as the dominant political form. Uniting at times into larger entities for greater protection against outside enemies such as the *Delian League* of ancient Greece, a union of several Greek city-states united against the power of ancient Persia.

Sometimes the union was effected by force, such as the *Pharaoh Menes,* uniting the lands of *Upper* and *Lower Egypt* into one *Kingdom of Egypt* around *3100 BC.* With the split and then fall, of the Roman Empire in the fourth century, the growth of any further large political entities in Europe was temporarily halted. The break up of the empire led to the establishment of very small units of political power being the only ones surviving the interim period of chaos and confusion. However also at this time the tribes that had originally fought the Romans now came to occupy the lands the Romans formerly controlled. Where the tribes had established themselves on the land, they became "united" out of sheer necessity against competing tribes. This in many cases extended little farther than appeals to a common kinship, language, and customs. In some sense, this was a burgeoning nationalism and it began to be felt in the various interrelationships amongst them.

This was also the time in which *Feudalism* as the dominant form of political organization arisen in Europe. Feudalism being the organization of people based on the ownership of land by a *Lord* or other *Noble* who allows individuals known as *peasants* or *serfs* to farm the land and to keep a portion of it. The lord or noble, in return for the serfs loyalty, offers them his protection. In practical effect, the serf is considered owned by his lord with little or no rights at all. The lord's sole obligation to the serfs is to protect them so they could continue to work for him (most, though not all lords were men). This system would last for many centuries. In Russia it would last until the 1860s.

Warfare among the various tribes would continue until **Charlemagne The Great** in the year 800 AD, united several of the larger tribes, such as the Germans and the Franks into the political entity known as the **Holy Roman Empire**. This entity would last in some form until 1806, but by then it had been replaced by the smaller entities, we know as modern states.

The final emergence of the nation-state is attributed to two principal causes. One major factor was the underlying fact of economic expansion that took place in the feudal system. This was mainly the result of a great expansion in trade and manufacturing which the creation of the Holy Roman Empire had helped to facilitate. The feudal system had been dependent on small, isolated, units and these were unable to cope with the great trade expansion, which was occurring. This gave rise to the system known as **Mercantilism**, a system in which certain lords started to take an interest in the growing merchant trade and used their power in order to facilitate it. This led to groups of powerful merchants gathering in the areas under the control of certain lords.

Thus, the various and independent feudal manors began to break up, leading to the growth of cities, expanded trade and the growth of markets up through the period that came to be known as the **Renaissance**. At the same time, (the 1500s) the **Protestant Reformation** was beginning. This would lead to the waning influence of the massive power and control of Catholic Church and allow the growth of various independent and powerful lords. As they began to control greater and greater areas of land, they became known as **kings**. They were now involving themselves in and profiting by, the growth in trade taking place. This is in contrast to the earlier feudal lords who had opposed the rise in trade and manufacturing as undermining their authority and power.

As the process continued, a split occurred in Europe at this time between those who still looked to the Catholic Church for guidance and the newly created and independent nation-states, which had by now had emerged and followed the new Protestant faith. This conflict would continue on and off, through many centuries and many wars, until the 19th century. Yet, even in those areas where the Catholic Church still had power and influence, a new sense of independence had emerged as well. The Church itself came to see the newly created states as a necessary factor in human affairs. Yet ever since the **Pope** had crowned Charlemagne as Emperor of the Holy Roman Empire, it has insisted, (and it has been granted in various ways), on its right to be considered above petty national considerations. Its' **religious** power being greater than the **secular** power of the state, an idea that in various forms and degrees has continued until our own day.

By the beginning of the 19th century, the state as we know it today had formed. A government claiming control over a specific area of land, uniting people of similar backgrounds and language, ruled either by some sort of monarch, or increasingly, by some sort of democratically elected government. The 19th century also saw the consolidation of several similar states into larger conglomerates, usually after some armed conflict such as the unification of the German States into one united nation in 1871 after the Franco-Prussian war.

By the 20th century, in the aftermath of the Second World War, the breakdown of colonial empires and the force of nationalism had become the dominant factor in world affairs, a factor that continues to grow in present time at an ever increasing rate, sometimes to the detriment of world peace and order.

Skill 5.3   Modern major philosophies of the nature of government

When looking at the modern major philosophies of the nature of government we will by necessity be looking at the works of men such as, **Niccolo Machiavelli, Thomas Hobbes, John Locke, Jean-Jacques Rousseau,** and **Karl Marx.**   Now this list is by no means exhaustive. However, in distinguishing political science from political philosophy, and by using the term "modern" in a broad sense, we will examine those thinkers whose works have had an actual practical effect on society, as opposed to simply trying to interpret human events. In other words, we will examine those ideas that people at different times have really tried to put into effect or have had in the end the longest lasting and widest influence.

Niccolo Machiavelli (1469-1527) One of the most important thinkers on politics and the nature of political power. His most famous work is *The Prince* (1532). In it, Machiavelli describes the means of gaining and holding onto political power. He looked at his work as a simple recitation of obvious facts. All political leaders want to stay in power, so very well, this is how you should do it. In reality, he was really describing the situation in his time. Nevertheless, his work has survived because it is a masterful piece that makes practical sense. A work that many a leader since has looked to as a guide for his or her own behavior. Throughout his career, Machiavelli had sought to describe a state that would be capable of resisting foreign attack and in maintaining internal order and discipline. His writings are concerned with the principles upon which such a state could be founded and with the means on which they can be implemented and maintained. In *The Prince*, he describes the method by which a "prince" (ruler) could acquire and maintain political power. This study has often been regarded as a defense of the despotism and tyranny of such rulers as Cesare Borgia (1476? -1507 Italian ruler). However, it is in actuality based on Machiavelli's belief that a ruler is not bound by traditional ethical norms. In his view, a prince should be concerned only with power and should be bound only by rules that would lead to success in political actions. Machiavelli believed that these rules could be discovered by deduction from the political practices of the time, as well as from those of earlier times. Specifically he used examples from ancient Greece and Rome and later times, seeing what worked and what did not, spelling out his theses in simple to understand and follow ideas. For instance, many of his classic quotes are:

"It is better to be feared than loved ... but one must strive not to be hated'.

"A prince need trouble little about conspiracies when the people are well disposed, but when they are hostile and hold him in hatred, then he must fear everything and everybody."

"A wise prince leaves his subjects their property, for a man will sooner forgive the death of his brother than the loss of his patrimony".

"A prince must show himself a lover of merit, give preferment to the able and honor those who excel in every ad'

"A man who wishes to make a profession of goodness in everything must necessarily come to grief among so many who are not good. Therefore, it is necessary ... to learn how not to be good, and to use this knowledge and not use it, according to the necessity of the case".

"The first impression that one gets of a ruler and of his brains is from seeing the men he has about him".

"There is no other way of guarding one's self against flattery than by letting men understand that they will not offend you by speaking the truth; but when every one can tell you the truth you lose their respect'.

"I certainly think that it is better to be impetuous than cautious, for fortune is a woman, and if it is necessary.. . to conquer her by force".

Thomas Hobbes (1588-1679*)* Author of the book **Leviathan** *(I651)* which was actually written as a reaction to the disorders caused by the English civil wars which had culminated with the execution of King Charles I. Hobbes perceived people as rational beings, but unlike Locke and Jefferson, he had no faith in their abilities to live in harmony with one another without a government. The trouble was, as Hobbes saw it, people were selfish and the strong would take from the weak. However, the weak being rational would in turn band together against the strong. For Hobbes, the state of nature became a chaotic state in which every person becomes the enemy of every other. It became a war of all against all, with terrible consequences for all. Hobbes wrote thus:

"In such condition there is no place for industry, because the fruit thereupon is uncertain and consequently no culture of the Earth; no navigation nor use of the commodities that may be imported by sea; no commodious building; no instruments of moving or removing such things as require much force; no knowledge of the face of the Earth; no account of time; no arts; no letters; no society; and which is worst of all, continual fear and danger of violent death; and the life of man solitary, poor, nasty, brutish, and short".

The solution proposed by Hobbes was for the citizens to enter a contract of "commonwealth" with one another. The conditions of the contract were that all of the citizens would agree to surrender all of their powers to a sovereign power, the *"Leviathan",* on condition that every other citizen would do so also. The Leviathan would then protect the citizens of the commonwealth and provide a system of law and order. In return, the citizens owed the Leviathan their absolute obedience. Thus there was only one agreement and to break it would mean the return of society to its uncivilized, chaotic past. The only reason for disobeying the leviathan then was if it failed in its main duty of protecting the society from disorder and protecting the life and property of the citizenry.

The interesting thing to remember is that Hobbes' aims were actually liberal in nature. He wanted to produce a society in which people would be free to advance and enjoy life. His lack of faith in their ability to govern themselves forced him to conclude that an absolute ruler was then necessary in order to bring about the desired liberal society.

John Locke (1632-1704) An important thinker on the nature of democracy. He regarded the mind of man at birth as a tabula rasa, a blank slate upon which experience imprints knowledge and behavior. He did not believe in the idea of intuition or theories of innate knowledge. Locke also believed that all men are born good, independent and equal. That it is their actions that will determine their fate. Locke's views, in his most important work, *Two Treatises of Civil Government* (1690) attacked the theory of the divine right of kings and the nature of the state as conceived by *Thomas Hobbes.* Locke argued that sovereignty did not reside in the state, but with the people. The state is supreme, but only if it is bound by civil and what he called "**natural**' law. Many of Locke's political ideas, such as those relating to natural rights, property rights, the duty of the government to protect these rights and the rule of the majority, were embodied in the Constitution of the United States. He further held that revolution was not only a right, but also often an obligation and advocated a system of checks and balances in government. A government comprised of three branches of which the legislative is more powerful than either the executive or the judicial. He also believed in the separation of the church and state. As is apparent all of these ideas were to be incorporated in the Constitution of the United States. As such Locke is considered in many ways the true founding father of our Constitution and government system. He remains one of history's most influential political thinkers to this day.

Jean-Jacques Rousseau (1712-1778), one of the most famous and influential political theorists before the French Revolution. His most important and most studied work is **The Social Contract** (1762). He was concerned with what should be the proper form of society and government. However, unlike Hobbes, Rousseau did not view the state of nature as one of absolute chaos. The problem as Rousseau saw it was that the natural harmony of the state of nature was due to people's intuitive goodness not to their actual reason. Reason only developed once a civilized society was established.

The intuitive goodness was easily overwhelmed however by arguments for institutions of social control, which likened rulers to father figures and extolled the virtues of obedience to such figures. To a remarkable extent, strong leaders have, in Rousseau's judgment, already succeeded not only in extracting obedience from the citizens that they ruled, but also more importantly, have managed to justify such obedience as necessary.

"Man is born free, and everywhere he is in chains"
This is one of Rousseau's most famous quotes from *"The Social Contract"* he also went on to state:

"The strongest is never strong enough to be always the master, unless he transforms his might into right and obedience into duty. Hence the right of the strongest, a right which looks like an ironical pleasantry, but in fact is a well-established principle".

However, Rousseau denied that might make right. The only authority which citizens ought to obey is a legitimate one and the only legitimate authority would be one which:

"Defends and protects the person and property of each member with the whole force of the community, and where each, while joining with all the rest, still obeys no one but himself..."

The solution as Rousseau saw it was the *"Social Contract',* a contract which does bear a strong resemblance to many of Hobbes' ideas. The main principle was that each individual gives up all of their rights, not just certain rights, to the community as a whole. Nevertheless, this community is not as independent a force as in Hobbes' "Leviathan", rather it is an expression of the "general will" of the citizens themselves. By means of it, each citizen becomes the subject of every act of government. The citizens in effect will give up their "primitive", or "natural" freedoms in exchange for the "higher" freedom to follow the general will. Rousseau also had a strong psychological as well as political purpose in his ideology. The governmental power he envisioned was one, which would not and could not harm the individual members of the community because it was composed of them.

Rousseau attempted to unite the individual citizen with the government in such a way, and with such a strong psychological bond that the citizen would submit to the general will. Although the people's private interest might seem to be contrary at times to the general will. At the same time, Rousseau wanted the submission of private interests to the general will to involve no real sacrifice. The general will represented what the citizen really wanted as a citizen of a community as opposed to what the citizen might want as a selfish individual.

In fact, if the whole community forced dissenters to conform to the general will, it would not bother Rousseau because to him such coercion of the individual *means nothing more or less than that he will be forced to be free"*.   For Rousseau, conformity to the general will was the highest form of freedom, obeying the general will was nothing more than obeying what was, in fact, actually the best for oneself.

Rousseau's most direct influence was upon the **French Revolution** (1789-1815*)*. In the **Declaration of the Rights of Man and The Citizen** (1789), it explicitly recognized the sovereignty of the general will as expressed in the law. In contrast to the American **Declaration of Independence**, it contains explicit mention of the obligations and duties of the citizen, such as assenting to taxes in support of the military or police forces for the common good. In modern times, ideas such as Rousseau's have often been used to justify the ideas of authoritarian and totalitarian systems.

Karl Marx (1818-1883), was perhaps the most influential theorist of the 19th century and his influence has continued in various forms until this day. Contrary to popular belief, he was not the first to believe in socialist ideas, many of which had been around for some time and in various forms. Nevertheless, he was the first to call his system truly "scientific" or "**Scientific Socialism**". (Also called Marxian Socialism or as it is more widely known Marxism).   It was opposed to other forms of socialism that had been called, (with some derision), "**Utopian Socialism**", (socialist ideas which though sounded good, nevertheless, would never really work in the real world). In fact, it is this very idea of Marxism being "scientific" that has been appealing to so many thinkers in modern history. (This and the underlying aspect of prophecy and redemption that is inherent, though seldom acknowledged, in Marxist ideology, has made it that much more attractive to those looking for something to believe in). Marx expounded his ideas in two major theoretical works, **The Communist Manifesto** (1848*)* and **Das Capital** ("Capital"), (vol.1 1867*)*.

Marx sought to combine historical analysis and political ideology in a thorough survey of the history of economic systems. Arguing that *"the history of all hitherto existing societies has been the history of class struggle"*, he believed that historically in all societies there has been a struggle between two different classes of people, the have and the have-nots. Alternatively, in the modern era, the owners and the workers, whom he called the **Bourgeoisie** and the **Proletariat**. Modern liberal governments and ideology are merely the agents of this class of exploiting owners of private property. Marx advocated the total abolition of private property and predicted the demise of the capitalist system after a series of recurring economic crisis. The abolition of private property and therefore of the exploitation of man by man, would make possible the situation known by the saying *"from each according to their abilities to each according to their needs"*. In which each individual would contribute to society according to their particular given ability and take according to their specific needs.

Marx believed that since the ruling class and the owners would never give up their position and power without a fight, that a violent revolution would be necessary in order to overthrow them. Once this was accomplished, a period of dictatorship known, as *"the dictatorship of the proletariat"* would then be necessary in order to sustain the new order while the struggle continued until the last of the exploiting classes were eliminated. Afterwards a new classless society would emerge. Without a class system, the state, which Marx said was created only to perpetuate this unequal and unfair class system, would then simply *"whither away"* creating a new just and perfect society.

Marx believed that this situation was inevitable because the modern era had seen these processes of struggle reach a crisis point, which simply could not continue. Capitalism had become the most efficient and terrible exploitative system yet devised. He believed that the exploitation of the working class would continue until a breaking point is reached and the workers rise in revolution.

Yet, a critical analysis of Marxism and history itself has shown the various forms of Marxian ideology to be false. What Marx had taken to be the death knell of capitalism was actually its' birth pangs. Far from leading to greater and greater exploitation capitalism after it had fully established, it actually began to lead to a gradual improvement in the standard of living for all classes over time. However, this was not apparent in the beginning. Instead of trying to continue to exploit the lower classes, the big owners and industrialists came to see them as partners in some ways. In other words, why manufacture goods if no one can buy them? Thus, it became important to allow the working class a standard of living high enough to enable them to become consumers and to purchase the products being produced. The spread of education, trade unionism and democracy also gradually led to the people gaining greater power and influence in society.

Therefore, as capitalism progressed instead of leading to a revolutionary condition, it led to the exact opposite situation. All classes in the society came to see that they had a stake in preserving the current institutions; reforming them if necessary but not ending them.

Where Marxism managed to gain any sort of great following, and attempted to carry out a revolution, was where capitalism was still in its' infancy. Its' worst features were still apparent and unchecked and where the spread of democratic ideals had been slowed as compared to other societies. For example, the Russian Revolution and its' attempt to create a Marxist system as well as China, and various small nations referred to as "third world countries".

In more advanced societies, Marxism changed from its previous revolutionary ideology into an evolutionary ideology. Owing to the fact that in these societies where democratic institutions had taken root along with capitalism, revolution was an extremely remote possibility if any. Yet, Marxists in these societies did believe that a socialist society was still desirable and inevitable, in the end. Thus a split occurred between those who still believed in the revolutionary idea, the Communists, and those who believed in the evolutionary path, the Democratic-Socialists. In most modern, democratic-capitalist societies socialism and socialist ideologies have not taken root in any large scale or meaningful way. At various times certain reformers and various reformist ideas, have in some ways and to varying degrees, incorporated ideas that can be considered to have socialist features. In all cases, they have been extremely limited in scope and in no way aimed at undoing the existing capitalist economic system, which is fundamental to the socialist belief system.

What has been achieved, and could be said to be a positive development from a socialist perspective, is the rise of what has been called "**The Welfare State**", or "**Welfare Capitalism**". These concepts have been most often used in regards to what has been called "post-capitalist society", which is what the United States and many Western European countries are called. These societies, though clinging to the basics of capitalism and free enterprise, have nevertheless adopted massive social programs, such as Social Security, unemployment insurance, and welfare. Measures aimed at easing some of the worst effects of capitalism. Thus, it can be said that socialism's triumph has been more in the breach, in its actual conceptions, as opposed to its outward forms. It is an interesting (and some might say perverse) fact that the apparent decrease in support of socialist ideology has been accomplished by the appropriation of these ideologies by the established order.

An underlying and often overlooked aspect of Marxism is its idealistic, **pseudo-religious** underpinnings. For all of its' claims to be "scientific", Marxism has much of the religious zeal in its' basic philosophy. It is this very fact that makes Marxism more of a belief system than a simple scientific theory. The belief is that a socialist, (whether revolutionary or reformist), is working for the greater good of humanity. Thus no actions to achieve this end, (especially to a communist), are proscribed. In other words "the end justifies the means", the end being no more human want and suffering. Thus any present day suffering is tolerated as being good for humanity in the long term. This is like the religious doctrine "a little suffering is good for the soul". This explains much of the often-violent history of some socialist movements (especially the communist variety). The fact that all of this human suffering has not brought the great future any closer has not stopped these ideas from continuing to be believed by some. In fact, this very pseudo-religious ideology has maintained the belief in socialism and communism.

This is also why in any comparison between socialist and capitalist economic forms, the socialists (especially the communists) are quick to point out that none of the existing societies that consider themselves "socialist", or "communist", have really achieved their goals. The real comparison they say is between what capitalism is and what socialism and communism should or will be. This by itself can be seen as being a facetious (not to mention completely unscientific) argument. It is like comparing the real world to an imagined utopia (a word that means "nowhere"). The fact that history has proved that in the real world this idealized, perfect society can never occur, **has not stopped these ideas from being believed** *by* **their adherents.**

In fact, with the fall of the Communist Eastern Bloc and experiments in capitalism and market forces in the remaining "communist" or "socialist" societies, Marxian socialist ideas (at least the revolutionary types), have thus generally fallen into disfavor. It is interesting to note that the only places they do continue to be thought about in any serious manner today is on the campuses of some American universities.

Skill 5.4   Other important modern political ideologies.

The other important modern political philosophies and ideologies that have had the greatest effect in the modern era are Socialism, Communism, and Fascism. Each will be examined in its turn. It might be interesting first, however, to look at a famous, though often misquoted-quoted saying comparing the ideas of Democracy (actually Social Democracy), Communism, and Fascism. It first originated in Germany in the 1930s prior to the rise of Hitler and was supposed to explain the different ideas that each political party represented and what each would entail in a humorous manner. In particular it was trying to explain how they operated:

*"What is the difference between the **Social-Democrats**, the **Communists**, and the **Fascists**?"*
*"Well, let's say that a farmer has six cows, under **Social-Democracy,** the government would take three, and leave the farmer three".*
"Under Communism, the government would take all six cows and leave the farmer nothing".
*"While the **Fascists** would leave the farmer all six cows, just so long as they got all the milk!"*

The three descriptions were actually trying to demonstrate the different economic approaches each respective ideology takes in regards to the means of production (in this case using cows as an example).

The Social Democrats would take some of the cows (in a strong **progressive tax** system) while leaving the farmer the rest.

The Communists, believing in the confiscation of all private property without compensation, at least in regards to the means of production, (a process called **nationalization**), would take all the cows and give the farmer nothing in return.

The Fascists according to their ideology, are against outright confiscation of private property and believe in allowing the means of production to remain in private hands, (this is one of its major historic appeals). Instead they are for strong economic control over society, thus they would allow the farmer to keep all of his cows, they would just insist on getting all of the production, in this case, the milk.

Of course, this is a simplified explanation for the differences between them, but it states the basics in a very concise and entertaining way. Now on to the specifics of the aforementioned ideologies:

Socialism - (see **Socialism**, Section 1.4 and **Karl Marx** Section 5.3) This is a recent political phenomenon, though its' roots can be traced far back in time in many respects. At the core, both socialism and communism are fundamentally economic philosophies that advocate public rather than private ownership especially over the means of production, yet even here, there are many distinctions. Karl Marx concentrated his attention on the industrial worker and on state domination over the means of production. In practice, this Marxian dogma has largely been followed the most in those countries that profess Communism in conjunction with massive programs for the development of heavy industry. This emphasis has been on production regardless of the wants or comforts of the individual in the given society. Socialism by contrast, usually occurring where industry has already been developed, has concerned itself more with the welfare of the individual and the fair distribution of whatever wealth is available.

Communism has a rigid theology and a bible *(Das Capital)* that sees Communism emerging as a result of almost cosmic laws. Modern socialism is much closer to the ground. It too sees change in human society and hopes for improvement, but there is no unchanging millennium at the end of the road. Communism is sure that it will achieve the perfect state and in this certainty, it is willing to use all means, however ruthless to bring it about. Socialism on the other hand, confident only that the human condition is always changing, makes no easy approximation between ends and means and so cannot justify brutalities. This distinction in philosophy of course makes for an immense conflict in methods. Communism believing that revolution is inevitable, works toward it by emphasizing class antagonisms, Socialism, while seeking change, insists on the use of democratic procedures within the existing social order of a given society. In it, the upper classes and capitalists are not to be violently overthrown but instead won over by logical persuasion.

It is interesting to note that in every perfect, idealized community or society that people have dreamed about throughout history, where human beings are pictured living in special harmony that transcends their natural instincts, there has been a touch of socialism. This tendency was especially found in the **Utopian-Socialists** of the early 19th century, whose basic aim was the repudiation of the private-property system with its economic inefficiency and social injustice. Their criticisms rather than any actual achievements would linger after them. Like Marx, they envisioned industrial capitalism as becoming increasingly inhumane and oppressive. They could not imagine the mass of workers prospering in such a system. Yet, the workers soon developed their own powerful organizations and institutions. They began to bend the economic system to their own benefit. Thus a split did occur.

First, between those who after the growing success of the labor movement rejected the earlier utopian ideas as being impractical. And those who saw in this new found political awareness of the working class the key to organizing a realistic ability of revolution, who saw this as inevitable based on their previous observations and study of history. Having reached a point where it has managed to jeopardize its very own survival, the inevitable revolution of those opposed to the present capitalist system had to occur. History has proven this so and history was always right and irrefutable.

These believers in the absolute correctness of this doctrine gathered around Marx in what he called **Scientific Socialism**, in contempt to all other kinds, which he considered scientific and therefore useless as a realistic political philosophy.

The next split would occur between those who believed in the inevitability of the coming revolution (the **Revolutionary Socialists**, or as they came to be known the **Communists**) and those who saw the growing political awareness of the working class. Accepting the basic idea that the current capitalist system could not last, the beginnings of an ability to effect peaceful and gradual change in the social order was beginning. They believed this is better in the end for everyone concerned as opposed to a cataclysmic, apocalyptic uprising, (The **Democratic-Socialists**).

 Major strides for the **Democratic-Socialists** were made before the First World War. A war that the Socialists, by philosophy pacifists, initially resisted, giving only reluctant support only when the struggle had begun. During the conflict, public sentiment against pacifism tended generally to weaken the movement, but with peace reaction set in. The cause of world socialism leaped forward, often overcompensating by adhering to revolutionary communism which in the **Revolution of 1917** had taken hold of in Russia. The period between the wars saw the sudden spurt of socialism. Whether their leanings were democratic or not, all socialists were bound together for a time in their resistance to fascism.

The decade following World War II saw tremendous growth in socialism. Economic planning and the nationalization of industry was undertaken in many countries and to this day has not been repudiated. A subsequent return to self-confidence in the private business community and among voters in general has frequently weakened the socialist majority or reduced it to the status of an opposition party. This political balance leaves most industrialized countries with a mixed socialist-capitalist economy. So long as there is no major worldwide depression, this situation may remain relatively stable. The consequences of World War II, particularly the independence of former European colonies has opened vast new areas for the attempted development of socialist forms. Most have tried to aspire to the democratic type, but very few have succeeded except where democratic traditions were strong.

Socialism, though concentrating on economic relationships, has always considered itself a complete approach to human society. In effect a new belief system and thus a world rather than a national movement. In this respect as well, it owes much to Great Britain for it was in London in 1864 that the first **Socialist International** was organized by Karl Marx. This radical leftist organization died off after limping along for twelve years, by which time its headquarters had moved to New York.

After the passage of about another twelve years the **Second Socialist International** met in Paris to celebrate the anniversary of the fall of the Bastille in the French Revolution. By this time, serious factions were developing. There were the Anarchists, (see Anarchism, Section 1.4), who wanted to tear down everything, Communists who wanted to tear down the established order and build another in its place, and the Democratic-Socialist majority who favored peaceful political action.

Struggling for internal peace and cohesion right up to the First World War, socialism would remain largely ineffectual at this critical international time.

Peace brought them all together again in Bern Switzerland, but by this time the Soviet Union had been created and the Russian Communists refused to attend the meeting on the grounds that the Second Socialist International opposed the type of dictatorship it saw as necessary in order to achieve revolutions. Thus, the **Communist International** was created in direct opposition to the Socialist International, while the socialists went on to advocate the "triumph of democracy, firmly rooted in the principles of liberty". The main objective of this new Socialist International was to maintain the peace, an ironic and very elusive goal in the period between the two world wars.

The Nazi attacks on Poland in September 1939 completely shattered the organization. In 1946, a new **Socialist Information and Liaison Office** was set up to reestablish old contacts, and in 1951, the International was revived with a conference in Frankfurt Germany, at which time it adopted a document entitled *"Aims and Tasks of Democratic Socialism".* A summary of these objectives gives a good picture of modern Democratic-Socialism as it exists on paper in its ideal form.

As always, the first principle is nationalized ownership of the major means of production and distribution. Usually public ownership is deemed appropriate for the strategically important services, public utilities, banking and resource industries such as coal, iron, lumber and oil. Farming has never been considered well adapted to public administration and has usually been excluded from nationalization. From this takeover of the free enterprise system socialists expect a more perfect freedom to evolve, offering equal opportunity for all, the minimizing of class conflict, better products for less cost, and security from physical want or need.

At the international level, socialism seeks a world of free peoples living together in peace and harmony for the mutual benefit of all. That freedom, at least from colonial rule, has largely been won. Peace throughout the world, however, is still as far off in most respects as it has ever been. However, according to the socialist doctrine, putting and end to capitalism will do much to reduce the likelihood of war. Armies and businesses are seen to need each other in a marriage of the weapons-mentality and devotion to private profit through the economic exploitation of weaker countries.

The United States remains the bastion of the free enterprise system. Socialism in the United States has long been regarded historically as a "menace" to the "American Way". There is no question that socialists do argue for change; capitalism in their opinion makes for unfair distribution of wealth, causing private affluence and public squalor. They also hold it responsible for environmental pollution and economic inflation. By curbing the absolute freedom of the private businessman or corporation, socialism hopes to satisfy all human necessities at the price of individual self-indulgence. Anti-trust legislation, the graduated income tax, and social security have all moved the United States toward the idea of the **"Welfare State"**, which recognizes as its prime objective full employment and a minimum living standard for all, whether employed or not. Even such taken for granted features of modern life as public schools and the federal postal service are relatively recent and socialistic innovations. Socialists applaud these programs, but, in what they regard as a sick society, these remedies seem to them only so much aspirin where major surgery is needed.

While communism and socialism arose in reaction to the excesses of 19th century capitalism, all three have matured in the past 100 years. Capitalism has mellowed, while a sibling rivalry may continue to exist between communism and socialism.

Officially, communism clings to the idea of revolution and the seizing of capitalist property by the state without compensation. Socialism accepts gradualism, feeling that a revolution, particularly in an industrial society would be ruinous. In fact, socialists and in some situations even communists, have come to realize that not all economic institutions function better in public hands. Private responsibility frequently offers benefits that go to the public good. This is particularly true in the agricultural sector, where personal ownership and cultivation of land have always been deeply ingrained.

All socialism denies certain freedoms, sometimes hidden in what it considers favorable terms. It deprives the minority of special economic privileges for the benefit of the majority. The more left wing, communistic socialism may deny the democratic process entirely. Traditionally defined democracy holds to the idea that the people, exercising their majority opinion at the polls, will arrive at the common good by electing representative individuals to govern them. Communists would interpret this to mean the tyranny of an uneducated majority obliged to decide between a politically selected group of would-be leaders.

There is no question that the democratic process has its limitations, but for want of a better method, contemporary socialism accepts democracy as a major principle.

The expressed goals of modern socialism are commendable, but goals of course are easy to state, especially when there is no real opportunity to carry them out in fact. The gulf between theory and practice is often insurmountable, the situation thus remains whether given the chance socialism can bring about a better world than now exists. Nowhere today does socialism exists in a pure and unchallenged form, but in many nations, it has made impressive gains.

Communism - (see "Communism", Section 1.4) is, in fact, a direct outgrowth of socialism. In 1848, Karl Marx (with Freidrich Engels) began his ***Communist Manifesto*** with the prophetic sentence *"a specter is haunting Europe, the specter of communism"*. Little more than a century later nearly one third of the world's population would live under governments professing communism, even with the collapse of the Soviet Union and the Eastern Communist Bloc. China with nearly one fourth of the world's population, not to mention North Korea and Cuba, still claim to follow the communist ideal. Yet, in even these societies, not one of them could say that they have achieved (through massive toil, treachery and bloodshed) the ideal state that communism was supposed to create.

Marx took the name for his ideal society from the ***French Communes***, feudal villages that held land and produce in common. However, he was not satisfied with villages, his dream was of a newly industrialized Europe shaped into a communist world. As he saw it, other systems would give way, or if they fought back, would be destroyed. With the birth of the industrial age in the early 19th century, privately owned factories employed larger and larger work forces. The owners of these factories made vast profits, which they plowed back into building more factories.

The workers were becoming mere tools in a huge anonymous crowd, alienated from the product of their toil. Labor was hard, often dangerous, and poorly rewarded. This was the economic system of capitalism in its formative years and Maw saw it leading only to increased enrichment of the owners of great businesses and to the eventual enslavement of the working class. Marx exhorted the workers to revolt. He urged them in his writings to seize the factories from the capitalists, not to become capitalist themselves, but in order to place the means of production in the hands of the community for the benefit of all its citizens. This intermediate society controlling the means of production is called the *"Dictatorship of the Proletariat"*. It is what the Soviet- Union and other so-called communist nations achieved, but it is *not* communism. True communism comes only with the further step of the state giving ownership back to the people. Who then continue to live together in abundance without supervision from a ruling class.

Pure Communism does not do now (in those few countries that still professes it), nor has it ever, existed in fact. Perhaps it never will. It is a never-never land of absolute bliss; heaven on Earth, the Garden of Eden revisited, this time for all to enjoy.

So, despite endless writing on the subject of communism, almost all of its verbiage has been devoted to the struggle to achieve socialism. Today for the commissar who drives the worker and the peasant who pulls the load, communism remains the goal, the end of the struggle. Though Marx and his disciples have insisted and continue to insist that socialism is only a stop on the way to communism, they have not dared to describe this final paradise on Earth except in the haziest of ways.

With the final achievement of communism, greed and competition will presumably cease. Individuals will contribute according to their ability and receive according to their need. There will be no cause for crime or vice of any kind, no race or class rivalry, no grounds for war and no reason for government.

Perfection indeed, but unhappily not yet of this world. In fact, it is measurably no nearer today anywhere than when Marx first conceived it.

As been examined earlier, the fact that it can never really occur has not stopped it from being believed in some quarters.

Fascism – The last important historical economic system to arise. It has been called a reaction against the last two ideologies discussed. It can at times cooperate with a Monarchy if it has to.

In general, Fascism is the effort to create, by dictatorial means, a viable national society in which competing interests were to be adjusted to each other by being entirely subordinated to the service of the state. The following features have been characteristic of Fascism in its various manifestations: **(1)** An origin at a time of serious economic disruption and of rapid and bewildering social change. **(2)** A philosophy that rejects democratic and humanitarian ideals and glorifies the absolute sovereignty of the state, the unity and destiny of the people, and their unquestioning loyalty and obedience to the dictator. **(3)** An aggressive nationalism which calls for the mobilization and regimentation of every aspect of national life and makes open use of violence and intimidation. **(4)** The simulation of mass popular support, accomplished by outlawing all but a single political party and by using suppression, censorship, and propaganda. **(5)** A program of vigorous action including economic reconstruction, industrialization, pursuit of economic self-sufficiency, territorial expansion and war which is dramatized as bold, adventurous, and promising a glorious future.

Fascist movements often had socialists origins. For example, in Italy, where fascism first arose in place of socialism, **Benito Mussolini**, sought to impose what he called "*corporativism*". A fascist "*corporate*" state would, in theory, run the economy for the benefit of the whole country like a corporation. It would be centrally controlled and managed by an elite who would see that its benefits would go to everyone.

Fascism has always declared itself the uncompromising enemy of communism, with which, however, fascist actions have much in common. (In fact, many of the methods of organization and propaganda used by fascists were taken from the experience of the early Russian communists, along with the belief in a single strong political party, secret police, etc.) The propertied interests and the upper classes, fearful of revolution, often gave their support to fascism on the basis of promises by the fascist leaders to maintain the status quo and safeguard property. (In effect, accomplishing a revolution from above with their help as opposed from below against them. However, fascism did consider itself a revolutionary movement of a different type).

Once established, a fascist regime ruthlessly crushes communist and socialist parties as well as all democratic opposition. It regiments the propertied interests to its national goals and wins the potentially revolutionary masses to fascist programs by substituting a rabid nationalism for class conflict. Thus fascism may be regarded as an extreme defensive expedient adopted by a nation faced with the sometimes illusionary threat of communist subversion or revolution. Under fascism, capital is regulated as much as labor and fascist contempt for legal or constitutional guarantees effectively destroyed whatever security the capitalistic system had enjoyed under pre-fascist governments.

In addition, fascist or similar regimes are at times anti-Communist. This is evidenced by the Soviet-German treaty of 1939. During the period of alliance created by the treaty, Italy and Germany, and their satellite countries ceased their anti-Communist propaganda. They emphasized their own revolutionary and proletarian origins and attacked the so-called plutocratic western democracies.

The fact that fascist countries sought to control national life by methods identical to those of communist governments make such nations vulnerable to communism after the fascist regime is destroyed.

In theory at least, the chief distinction between fascism and communism is fascism is **nationalist**, exalting the interests of the state and glorifying war between nations. Whereas, communism is **internationalist**, exalting the interests of a specific economic class (the proletariat) and glorifying world wide class warfare. In practice, however, this fundamental distinction loses some of its validity. For in its heyday, fascism was also an internationalist movement. A movement dedicated to world conquest, (like communism), as evidenced by the events prior to and during the Second World War. At the same time, many elements in communism as it evolved came to be very nationalistic as well.

Theoretically, communist systems are to follow "Democratic - centralism." People elect officials to elect higher party organizations, which in turn elect higher officials and finally appoint a chairman or general secretary. In practice however all communist systems work the opposite whereby party leaders appoint all officials.

In a fascist system, no pretense of Democratic ideals is observed. The leader is idealized as the supreme ruler with absolute power over the entire state. The leader thus appoints and demotes officials at will. The party is seen as an expression of the leaders will.

Competency 6.0   Knowledge of factors affecting politics

Skill 6.1   The influence of geography, economics, and culture on politics

Many different factors affect and influence politics, of them **geography**, **economics** and **culture** are among the most important. Looking at geography, we should realize that the geographic location of a particular country (that is the type of politics we will examine, those that take place on a national level) would greatly affect its' politics. Both domestic and foreign policy is determined by a given country's location. For instance, in an area like Europe where there are many independent countries in close proximity to each other, the development of rivalries and conflicts was bound to arise. The main struggle would be over boundaries and control of the limited amount of land that is available for each national group. We can see historically how these conflicts have arisen throughout history whenever two or more countries that are in close proximity to each other engage in warfare. It is a fact of human experience that a majority of wars throughout history has begun for the most part over the issue of land, later spreading to other lands in a continuing competition.

In fact, if we examine the history of European colonialism, we see that the struggle for empires and land overseas was a direct result and outgrowth of the inability for expansion for the relief of growing population and economic pressures.

In a country like the United States for instance, separate for the most part from other nations by the wide oceans, the chances for conflict is that much greatly diminished. In the case of the United States, it started small as colonies established along a wide coast. With its' independence, it had the ability to expand throughout a large land area straight across to the other side of the continent. This has been the most important fact in both America's growth from small, lightly populated former colonies, to the strongest major power in the world. The policies of every American administration since independence have also focused on this idea, the right and obligation for America to expand and control the entire area between its two coasts. An idea called "**Manifest Destiny**" or its "obvious" destiny, (see Manifest Destiny Section 1.1). The fact that this massive expansion was able to occur with little or no real conflict helped it in the extent and speed by which it did occur.

The ability of America to expand so much so fast was directly related to its having no real enemies or rivals for power on the continent. The native Indian populations were too unorganized and too weak to be able to stop it. In addition, the European powers were similarly forced out of the continent, a process that accelerated with defeat of Great Britain in the American Revolution. With America's growing power, it was able to proclaim the "**Monroe Doctrine**", (see Monroe Doctrine Section 1.1), that told the Europeans that they will stay out of this area of the world. The only other countries that could possibly compete with the United States for hegemony on this continent, Mexico and Canada, are much less strong than the United States. Canada was then a semi-colony of Great Britain, even after it gained most of its independence. It remained sparsely populated and in any case, it has a similar culture and a similar economy to the United States. It also has a large area of uninhabited land in which to develop. The only other power in this hemisphere, Mexico, poses no real problem for the United States. Though there was a conflict with Mexico in the middle of the 1800s over land issues owing to America's expansionist policy, it was no real contest. America was and remains a stronger nation than Mexico.

This is a legacy of both Mexico's pre-colonial history and its' history as a Spanish colony which did not allow it to develop along similar lines to the United States. Though it has a large land area, a large population and some important natural resources like oil, the fact that America constantly was acquiring more and more land, with relatively little cost was a factor in its *internal* stability.

Americans had no basis for conflict with each other. With no history of Feudalism or class conflict, plus a wide open country with a lot of available cheap land, Americans who did not like their present circumstances could, in the words of the writer Horace Greeley, simply *"go West'.*

This they did in ever larger and larger numbers with assistance from the government, which made such settlement of newly acquired land easy and cheap. Most other nations did not enjoy this luxury. This pioneering spirit free of class conflict and violence, with peaceful borders and relative isolation goes a long way in explaining the ability of America to become the strongest economic and military power on the Earth. The lack of area in which to expand uncontested is what has lead to continual strife in other countries of the world, most notably and with the most serious consequences, in Europe.

The history of warfare in Europe can be directly traced to this basic conflict over land especially among the great European powers, Germany, France, Russia and Italy.

Great Britain is also considered a great European power although it has no land borders with Europe. In fact, because of its close proximity to the European continent and its vulnerability to invasion, the one constant in British foreign policy has been to keep any one power from gaining hegemony in Europe. That is why Britain went to war against Napoleon and why it got involved in World War I and World War II.

Throughout history, thus, we see geographic location has been of supreme importance. It has been a major factor in a nation's ability to advance its interests, even in the modern era and looking at continuing world events this fact is not likely to change.

Looking at **economics** - we must consider what is known as **Political Economy**, that is the interrelationship between politics and economics. They are closely tied together. In fact, it has been stated by many different theorists that politics itself is just the particular method that people have adapted in order to solve their economic problems.

Among the most prominent of these has been Karl Marx (see "**Karl Marx**' Section 5.3, "Socialism" Section 5.4, "**Communism**" Section 5.4).

Other important theorists on how politics and economics interact are **Adam Smith** and his most famous work, "***The Wealth of Nations***" (1776). In it, he promoted the idea of "**Laissez Faire**", or letting an economy run itself with little or no government interference.

Also important was **Thomas Malthus**, who wrote about population problems over available food, land, and resources.

John Maynard Keynes who studied the business cycle and gave rise to an economic theory that bears his name.

The most important fact in economics is the question of the ordering of the economy, and as stated, politics is how the economy is set up. Two of the most prominent methods is the **market** and **central planning**. The market is most closely associated with democratic free enterprise as is practiced in the United States. Central planning is an important feature of socialist, communist and to an extent fascist system. Whatever system is in place, all economies have to answer the basic questions of what to produce, how to produce it, and for whom to produce it.

Calvin Coolidge once said, "the business of America is business". He may have been overstating it but generally, this can be said to be true and not only for the United States but also more and more for all nations.

The third major component we will examine in politics is **culture**. Though it may be examined third, it is by no means third in importance. In fact, all three things we are examining can be, at times of equal importance. The first two, **geography** and **economics**, are more or less external forces. People choose (usually) the type of government and what type of economic policy they will follow.

In addition, a country can try to *lessen geographic pressure*. This can be done by staying neutral like Switzerland, or by maintaining superior and powerful armed forces capable of repelling aggression directed against it like Israel. A nation with no strategic geographic territory in an area where it is outnumbered, out gunned, and surrounded by aggressive neighbors. Its survival has been a matter of sheer superior capabilities.

Alternatively, a nation can simply be fortunate to live with large oceans for borders like the United States.

However, a nation's culture is something that is immutable and intrinsically a part of a people. Thus, all of its politics will be naturally defined by it. The fact is that all peoples are different from each other. This is not a value judgment; it is not a question of superiority, or inferiority. Terms like "**Social Darwinism**" (the struggle among peoples in which only the strong survive) or "**White Man's Burden**" the presumed justification for colonial expansion have historically been used to justify ideas of national or cultural superiority. (The white Europeans felt they had a burden or obligation to "civilize" the world).

However, culture simply means those attitudes and beliefs that a nation holds that affects their political and economic decisions. It is a fact of history that at certain times specific peoples and cultures have found themselves in positions of importance or power that gave them an advantage over others. Usually this is because those cultures found themselves *better able to adapt to changing circumstances and times.* Examples of cultures that maximized their advantages have been the Roman Empire, Great Britain, Germany, Japan, and the United States. Each one of these arose from simple beginnings to positions of immense power in the world. This is directly traceable to their cultures, which proved themselves up to the challenges they were presented with. The keyword historically for success thus is *adaptability*.

Competency 7.0   *Knowledge of different governmental systems*

Skill 7.1   **Contrasting democracy, totalitarianism and authoritarianism**

The differences between democracy vs. totalitarianism and authoritarianism are an easier comparison to make since most understand the general differences, if not the specifics. While the differences between **_totalitarianism_** and **_authoritarianism_** is not as readily apparent, indeed most do not understand that there is a difference. That being the case, on the political spectrum democracy stands on one side and totalitarianism and authoritarianism both stand on the other. We will consider the differences between those two first. The difference between the two of them and democracy is in actuality a very great difference between totalitarianism and authoritarianism. That is why there are two different expressions, they are names for two different ideas, and that is where we will start.

Consider the two names. We see that totalitarianism is derived from the word *total*, while authoritarianism is derived from the word *authority*. The essential idea is that while many may use the two expressions together and interchangeably, in regards to political movements such as Fascism, Communism, and similar types of regimes, there are really two different ideas. The difference is that a *totalitarian* system doesn't recognize the right for any aspect of society to be outside the influence of the state. Such a government sees itself as having a legitimate concern with all levels of human existence. Not only in regards to freedom of speech, or press, but even to social and religious institutions it tries to achieve a complete conformity to its ideals. Thus, those ideologies that presume to speak to all of society's ills, such as communism and fascism, look to this model for what they attempt to create in society. As Benito Mussolini said "*nothing outside of the state, nothing instead of the state*".

Those regimes that conform to the **authoritarian** model never presume to seek such a complete reordering of society. Thus, those dictatorships that arise without this social pretentious can best be described as authoritarian. They do usually leave some autonomous institutions, such as the Church, alone as long as they do not interfere with the state authority. This model can be seen in the history of Central and South America, where regimes, usually representing the interests of the upper classes, came to power and instituted dictatorships that seek to concentrate all political power in a few hands. While at the same time, no overall embracing ideology of control is even thought about, let alone attempted. This is seen in many of these countries. The Church soon becomes an institution of opposition to the state authority. After an initial period of acceptance, if the state was originally seen as providing order in the society and fighting communism. The only regimes where the drive for total society changing control was attempted was in those regimes in Cuba and Nicaragua that held to the Marxist-Communist world view.

Democracy is a much more familiar system to most. In the United States, it is the system under which we live. The term comes from the Greek "for the rule of the people" and that is just what it is. The two most prevalent types are ***direct*** and ***indirect*** democracy, (see ***Direct Democracy*** and ***Indirect Democracy***, Section 1.1). Direct democracy usually involves all the people in a given area coming together to vote and decide on issues that will affect them. It is used only when the population involved is relatively small, for instance a local town meeting. An **indirect democracy** involves much larger areas and populations and involves the sending of representatives to a legislative body to vote on issues affecting the people. Such a system can be comprised of a ***Presidential*** or ***Parliamentary*** system (see Section 1.3).   In the United States, we follow an indirect, or representative democracy of the presidential type.

Competency 8.0   The American political system

Skill 8.1   The influence of the Magna Carta, Petition of Right, and the British Bill of Rights

The Magna Carta - This charter has been considered the basis of English constitution liberties. It was granted to a representative group of English barons and nobles on *June 15, 1215* by the British King John, after they had forced it on him. The English barons and nobles sought to limit what they had come to perceive as the overwhelming power of the Monarchy in public affairs. The Magna Carta is considered to be the first modern document that sought to try to limit the powers of the given state authority. It guaranteed feudal rights, regulated the justice system, and abolished many abuses of the King's power to tax and regulates trade. It said that the king could not raise new taxes without first consulting a Great Council, made up of nobles, barons, and Church people. Significantly the Magna Carta only dealt with the rights of the upper classes of the nobility and all of its provisions excluded the rights of the common people. However, gradually the rights won by the nobles were given to other English people. The Great Council grew into a representative assembly called the Parliament. By the 1600s, Parliament was divided into the House of Lords, made up of nobles and the House of Commons. Members of the House of Commons were elected to office. In the beginning, only a few wealthy men could vote. Still English people firmly believed that the ruler must consult Parliament on money matters and obey the law. Thus, it did set a precedent that there was a limit to the allowed power of the state. A precedent, which would have no small effect on the history of political revolution, is notably the American Revolution.

The Petition of Right - In English history, it was the title of a petition that was addressed to the King of England *Charles I,* by the British parliament in **1628**. The Parliament demanded that the king stop proclaiming new taxes without its' consent. Parliament demanded that he cease housing soldiers and sailors in the homes of private citizens, proclaiming martial law in times of peace, and that no subject should be imprisoned without a good cause being shown. After some attempts to circumvent these demands, Charles finally agreed to them. They later had an important effect on the demands of the revolutionary colonists, as these were some of the rights that as Englishmen, they felt were being denied to them. It Petition of Right was also the basis of specific protections that the designers of the Constitution made a point of inserting in the document.

British Bill of Rights - Also known as the *Declaration of Rights*, it spelled out the rights that were considered to belong to Englishmen. It was granted by *King William III* in 1869. It had previously been passed by a convention of the Parliament and it came out of the struggle for power that took place in Great Britain and at that time and was known as *The Glorious Revolution*. It was known as a revolution that was accomplished with virtually no bloodshed and led to King William III and Queen Mary II becoming joint sovereigns.

The Declaration itself was very similar in style to the later American Bill of Rights. It protected the rights of individuals and gave anyone accused of a crime the right to trial by jury. It outlawed cruel punishments; also, it stated that a ruler could not raise taxes or an army without the consent of Parliament. The colonists as Englishmen were protected by these provisions. The colonists considered abridgments of these rights that helped to contribute to the revolutionary spirit of the times.

All of these events and the principles that arose from them are of the utmost importance in understanding the process that eventually led to the ideals that are inherent in the Constitution of the United States. In addition, the fact is that all of these ideals are universal in nature and have become the basis for the idea of human freedoms throughout the world.

Skill 8.2   The influence of the Declaration of Independence and the Articles of Confederation

Declaration of Independence - The Declaration of Independence was the founding document of the United States of America. The Articles of Confederation were the first attempt of the newly independent states to reach a new understanding amongst themselves. The Declaration was intended to demonstrate the reasons that the colonies were seeking separation from Great Britain. Conceived by and written for the most part by Thomas Jefferson, it is not only important for what it says, but also for how it says it. The Declaration is in many respects a poetic document. Instead of a simple recitation of the colonists' grievances, it set out clearly the reasons why the colonists were seeking their freedom from Great Britain. They had tried all means to resolve the dispute peacefully. It was the right of a people, when all other methods of addressing their grievances have been tried and failed, to separate themselves from that power that was keeping them from fully expressing their rights to "**life, liberty, and the pursuit of happiness**".

Articles of Confederation - This was the first political system under which the newly independent colonies tried to organize themselves. It was drafted after the Declaration of Independence, in 1776, was passed by the Continental Congress on November 15, 1777, ratified by the thirteen states, and took effect on March 1, 1781.

The newly independent states were unwilling to give too much power to a national government. They were already fighting Great Britain. They did not want to replace one harsh ruler with another. After many debates, the form of the Articles was accepted. Each state agreed to send delegates to the Congress. Each state had one vote in the Congress. The Articles gave Congress the power to declare war, appoint military officers, and coin money. The Congress was also responsible for foreign affairs. The Articles of Confederation limited the powers of Congress by giving the states final authority.

Although Congress could pass laws, at least nine of the thirteen states had to approve a law before it went into effect. Congress could not pass any laws regarding taxes. To get money, Congress had to ask each state for it, no state could be forced to pay.

Thus, the Articles created a loose alliance among the thirteen states. The national government was weak, in part, because it didn't have a strong chief executive to carry out laws passed by the legislature. This weak national government might have worked if the states were able to get along with each other. However, many different disputes arose and there was no way of settling them. Thus, the delegates went to meet again to try to fix the Articles; instead they ended up scrapping them and created a new Constitution that learned from these earlier mistakes.

They created a government that as Benjamin Franklin said, *"though it may not be the best there is"*; he said that he, *"wasn't sure that it could be possible to create one better"*. A fact that might be true considering that the Constitution has lasted, through civil war, foreign wars, depression, and social revolution for over 200 years.

It is truly a living document because of its ability to remain strong while allowing itself to be changed with changing times.

Skill 8.3   The philosophical basis of the Declaration of Independence

The Declaration of independence is an outgrowth of both ancient Greek ideas of democracy and individual rights and the ideas of the European Enlightenment and the Renaissance, especially the ideology of the political thinker *John Locke*. Thomas Jefferson (1743-1826) the principle author of the Declaration borrowed much from Locke's theories and writings *(See John Locke Section 5.3)*.

Essentially, Jefferson applied Locke's principles to the contemporary American situation. Jefferson argued that the currently reigning King George III had repeatedly violated the rights of the colonists as subjects of the British Crown. Disdaining the colonial petition for redress of grievances (a right guaranteed by the Declaration of Rights of 1689), the King seemed bent upon establishing an "absolute tyranny" over the colonies. Such disgraceful behavior itself violated the reasons for which government had been instituted. The American colonists were left with no choice, *"it is their right, it is their duty, to throw off such a government, and to provide new guards for their future security"* so wrote Thomas Jefferson.

Yet, though his fundamental principles were derived from Locke's, Jefferson was bolder than his intellectual mentor was. He went farther in that his view of natural rights was much broader than Locke's and less tied to the idea of property rights.

For instance, though both Jefferson and Locke believed very strongly in property rights, especially as a guard for individual liberty, the famous line in the Declaration about people being endowed with the inalienable right to "life, liberty and the pursuit of happiness", was originally Locke's idea. It was "life, liberty, and *private property"*. Jefferson didn't want to tie the idea of rights to any one particular circumstance however, thus, he changed Locke's original specific reliance on property and substituted the more general idea of human happiness as being a fundamental right that is the duty of a government to protect.

Locke and Jefferson both stressed that the individual citizen's rights are prior to and more important than any obligation to the state. Government is the servant of the people. The officials of government hold their positions at the sufferance of the people. Their job is to ensure that the rights of the people are preserved and protected by that government. The citizen come first, the government comes second. The Declaration thus produced turned out to be one of the most important and historic documents that expounded the inherent rights of all peoples; a document still looked up to as an ideal and an example.

Skill 8.4   **Overview of the duties, responsibilities and powers of each branch of the government**

In the United States, the three branches of the federal government: the **Executive**, the **Legislative**, and the **Judicial** divide their powers thus:

Legislative - Article I of the Constitution established the legislative, or law-making branch of the government called the Congress. It is made up of two houses, the House of Representatives and the Senate. Voters in all states elect the members who serve in each respective house of Congress. The Legislative branch is responsible for making laws, raising and printing money, regulating trade, establishing the postal service and federal courts, approving the President's appointments, declaring war and supporting the armed forces. The Congress also has the power to change the Constitution itself and to impeach (bring charges against) the President. Charges for impeachment are brought by the House of Representatives and are tried in the Senate .

Executive – Article II of the Constitution created the Executive branch of the government, headed by the President, who leads the country, recommends new laws, and can veto bills passed by the Legislative branch. As the chief of state, the President is responsible for carrying out the laws of the country and the treaties and declarations of war passed by the Legislative branch. The President also appoints federal judges and is Commander in Chief of the military when it is called into service. Other members of the Executive branch include the Vice-President, also elected. Various cabinet members as he might appoint, ambassadors, presidential advisers, members of the armed forces, and other appointed and civil servants of government agencies, departments and bureaus.

Though the President appoints them, they then must be approved by the legislative branch.

Judicial - Article III of the Constitution established the Judicial branch of government headed by the Supreme Court. The Supreme Court has the power to rule that a law passed by the Legislature, or an act of the Executive branch is illegal and unconstitutional (See *Judicial Review,* Section 1.2). In an appeal capacity, citizens, businesses, and government officials can also ask the Supreme Court to review a decision made in a lower court if someone believes that the ruling by a judge is unconstitutional. The Judicial branch also includes lower federal courts known as federal district courts that have been established by the Congress. The courts try lawbreakers and review cases refereed from other courts.

Skill 8.5   Understanding the ideas of delegated, implied, reserved, and concurrent powers of the federal government and states

Powers delegated to the federal government:

1. To tax.
2. To borrow and coin money
3. To establish postal service.
4. To grant patents and copyrights.
5. To regulate interstate and foreign commerce.
6. To establish courts.
7. To declare war.
8. To raise and support the armed forces.
9. To govern territories.
10. To define and punish felonies and piracy on the high seas.
11. To fix standards of weights and measures.
12. To conduct foreign affairs.

Powers reserved to the states:

1. To regulate intrastate trade.
2. To establish local governments.
3. To protect general welfare.
4. To protect life and property.
5. To ratify amendments.
6. To conduct elections.
7. To make state and local laws.

Concurrent powers of the federal government and states.

1. Both Congress and the states may tax.
2. Both may borrow money.
3. Both may charter banks and corporations.
4. Both may establish courts.
5. Both may make and enforce laws.
6. Both may take property for public purposes.
7. Both may spend money to provide for the public welfare.

Implied powers of the federal government.

1. To establish banks or other corporations implied from delegated powers to tax, borrow, and to regulate commerce.
2. To spend money for roads, schools, health, insurance, etc. implied from powers to establish post roads, to tax to provide for general welfare and defense, and to regulate commerce.
3. To create military academies, implied from powers to raise and support an armed force.
4. To locate and generate sources of power and sell surplus implied from powers to dispose of government property, commerce, and war powers.
5. To assist and regulate agriculture, implied from power to tax and spend for general welfare and regulate commerce.

Skill 8.6   The role and development of political parties in the United States.

In regards to the American political system, it is important to realize that political parties are never mentioned in the United States Constitution. In fact, George Washington himself warned against the creation of "factions" in American politics, that cause "jealousies and false alarms", and the damage they could cause to the body politic. Thomas Jefferson echoed this warning, yet he would come to lead a party himself.

Americans had good reason to fear the emergence of political parties; they had witnessed how parties worked in Great Britain. Parties, called **"factions"** in Britain, thus Washington's warning, were made up of a few people who schemed to win favors from the government. They were more interested in their own personal profit and advantage than in the public good. Thus, the new American leaders were very interested in keeping factions from forming. However, it was ironically disagreements between two of Washington's chief advisors, Thomas Jefferson and Alexander Hamilton that, in fact, spurred the formation of the first political parties in the newly formed United States of America.

The two parties that developed through the early 1790s were led by Jefferson as the Secretary of State and Alexander Hamilton as the Secretary of the Treasury. Jefferson and Hamilton were different in many ways. Not the least was their views on what should be the proper form of the government of the United States. This difference helped to shape the parties that formed around them.

Hamilton wanted the federal government to be stronger than the state governments. Jefferson believed that the state governments should be stronger. Hamilton supported the creation of the first Bank of the United States; Jefferson opposed it, because he felt that it gave too much power to wealthy investors who would help run it. Jefferson interpreted the Constitution strictly, he argued that nowhere did the Constitution give the federal government the power to create a national bank. Hamilton interpreted the Constitution much more loosely. He pointed out that the Constitution gave the Congress the power to make all laws "necessary and proper" to carry out its duties. He reasoned that since the Congress had the right to collect taxes, then the Congress had the right to create the bank. Hamilton wanted the government to encourage economic growth. He favored the growth of trade, manufacturing and the rise of cities as the necessary parts of economic growth. He favored the business leaders and mistrusted the common people.

Jefferson believed that the common people, especially the farmers, were the backbone of the nation. He thought that the rise of big cities and manufacturing would corrupt American life.

Finally, Hamilton favored Great Britain, an important trading partner of the United States, (even after the Revolution). Jefferson favored France, America's first ally and a nation whose people were at that time involved in their own revolution.

At first, Hamilton and Jefferson had their disagreements only in private. But when the Congress began to pass many of Hamilton's ideas and programs, Jefferson and his friend James Madison, decided to organize support for their own views. They moved quietly and very cautiously in the beginning. In 1791, they went to New York telling people that they were going to study its' wildlife. Actually, Jefferson was more interested in meeting with several important New York politicians such as its governor George Clinton and Aaron Burr, a strong critic of Hamilton. Jefferson asked Clinton and Burr to help defeat Hamilton's program by getting New Yorkers to vote for Jefferson's supporters in the next election. Before long, leaders in other states began to organize support for either Jefferson or Hamilton. Jefferson's supporters called themselves **Democratic-Republicans** (often this was shortened just to Republicans, though in actuality it was the forerunner of today's Democratic Party, not the Republican Party). Hamilton and his supporters were known as the **Federalists**, because they favored a strong federal government. The Federalists had the support of the merchants and ship owners in the Northeast and some planters in the South. Small farmers, craft workers, and some of the wealthier landowners supported Jefferson and the Democratic-Republicans.

Newspapers, then as now, influenced the growth of political parties. Newspaper publishers and editors took sides on the issues. Thus, from the very beginning American newspapers and each new branch of the media have played an important role in helping to shape public opinion.

By the time Washington retired from office in 1796, the new political parties would come to play an important role in choosing his successor with each putting up its' own candidates for office. Thus, the election of 1796 was the first one in which political parties played a role. A role that, for better or worse, they have continued to play in various forms, in one way or another, for all of American history. By the beginning of the 1800s, the Federalist Party, torn by internal divisions, began suffering a decline. After the Election in 1800, of Thomas Jefferson, Hamilton's bitter rival, as President and after its' leader Alexander Hamilton was killed in 1804 in a duel with Aaron Burr, the Federalist party began to collapse. By 1816, after losing a string of important elections, (Jefferson was reelected in 1804 and James Madison a Democratic-Republican was elected in 1808) the Federalist Party ceased to be an effective political force and soon passed off the national stage.

By the late 1820s, new political parties had grown up. The Democratic Republican Party (or again simply the Republican Party) had been the major party for many years, but differences within it about the direction the country was headed in caused a split after 1824. Those who favored strong national growth took the name Whigs, after a similar party in Great Britain and united around then President John Quincy Adams. Many business people in the Northeast as well as some wealthy planters in the South supported it.

Those who favored slower growth and were more worker and small farmer oriented went on to form the new Democratic Party, with Andrew Jackson being its first leader as well as becoming the first President from it. It is the forerunner of today's present party of the same name.

In the mid-1850s, the slavery issue was beginning to heat up. In 1854, those opposed to slavery, the Whigs and some northern Democrats, united to form the Republican Party. (Before the Civil War, the Democratic Party was more heavily represented in the South and thus was pro-slavery for the most part). By the time of the Civil War, the present form of the major political parties had been formed. Though there would sometimes be drastic changes in ideology and platforms over the years, no other political parties would mange to gain enough strength to seriously challenge the "Big-Two" parties.

In fact, the two parties have shown themselves to adapt to changing times. In many instances, they have managed to shut out other parties by simply adapting their platforms. For example, in the 1930s during the Depression and in the years immediately proceeding it, the Democratic Party adapted much of the Socialist Party platform and under Franklin Roosevelt put much of it into effect. This managed to eliminate any contenders as a serious threat. Since the Civil War, no other political party has managed to either gain enough support to elect members to Congress or to elect a President. Some have come closer than others, but barring any unforeseen circumstances, the absolute monopoly on national political debate seems very secure in the hands of the Republican and Democratic parties.

Time will tell if this is to remain so. For history and political science teach us that the American people are quite willing to change their support from one area or group to another. Especially if it means a better way of doing things, or will give them more opportunity and freedoms. As conservative as some might think Americans have become there has always been and always will be something of the revolutionary spirit about them.

Skill 8.8   **Elements of democratic suffrage and elections in the United States**

The term **suffrage** means voting or the right to vote. Historically the right to vote had always been very limited, though elections have always been associated with democratic practices, various limitations has placed on the right to vote throughout history. These have included property qualifications, poll taxes, residency requirements, and restrictions against the right of women to vote.

In 1787, the Constitution of the United States provided for the election of the chief executive in Article II, Section I, and members of the national legislature in Article I, Section II. A number of election abuses, however, led to the adoption of what was known as the **Australian** or **secret ballot** and to the practice of registering voters prior to Election Day. Voting machines were first used in the United States in 1892. During the 19th century, the electorate in the United States grew considerably. Most of the states franchised all white male adults, although the so-called poll tax was retained, it was abolished by the **24th Amendment** to the Constitution ratified in 1964. The **15th Amendment** to the United States' Constitution ratified in 1870 extended the vote to the former black slaves. In the period after the Civil War known as Reconstruction, many blacks were elected to high office for the first time in American history. It was during the post-Civil War period that the primary system of selecting candidates for public office became widely used. By 1900, the system of primaries was regulated by law in most states. Women in the United States were granted the right to vote by the **19th Amendment** to the Constitution, which was ratified in 1920. The right to vote was extended to those eighteen years of age by the **26th Amendment** to the Constitution ratified in 1971.

The struggle over what is to be the fair method to ensure equal political representation for all different groups in the United States continues to dominate the national debate. This has revolved around the problems mostly of trying to ensure proper racial and minority representation. Various civil rights acts, notably the **Voting Rights Act of 1965**, sought to eliminate the remaining features of unequal suffrage in the United States. Most recently, the question has revolved around the issue of what is called "**Gerrymandering**", which involves the adjustment of various electoral districts in order to achieve a predetermined goal. Usually this is used in regards to the problem of minority political representation. This sometimes creates odd and unusual looking districts, (this is where the practice gets its name), and most often the sole basis of the adjustments is racial. In recent years, this has led to the questioning of this practice being fair, let alone constitutional, way in order for society to achieve its desired goals. This alone promises to be the major issue in national electoral politics for some time to come.

The debate has centered on those of the "left" (**Liberals**) who favor such methods and the "right", (**Conservatives**) who oppose them. Overall, most Americans would consider themselves in the "middle" (Moderates).

Competency 9.0   *Knowledge of the penal system*

Skill 9.1   **The jurisdiction of the court system at national and state levels**.

The Federal Court System - is provided for in the Constitution of the United States on the theory that the judicial power of the federal government could not be entrusted to the individual states, many of which had opposed the idea of a strong federal government in the first place. Thus Article III, Section 1, of the Constitution says: *"the judicial power of the United States shall be vested in one Supreme Court, and in such inferior courts as the Congress may from time to time ordain and establish"*. In accordance with these provisions, Congress passed the *Judiciary Act* in 1789, organizing the Supreme Court of the United States and establishing a system of federal courts of inferior jurisdiction. The states were left to establish their own judicial systems subject to the exclusive overall jurisdiction of the federal courts and to Article VI of the Constitution declaring the judges of the state courts to be bound to the Constitution and to the laws and treaties of the United States. Thus, developed in the United States a dual system of judicial power and authority.

The jurisdiction of the federal courts is further defined in Article III, Section 2 of the Constitution as extending in law and in equity to all cases arising under the Constitution and through federal legislation to controversies in which the United States is a party, including those arising from treaties with other governments, to maritime cases on the high seas in areas under American control, to disagreements between the states, between a citizen and a state, between citizens in different states and between a citizen and a foreign nation. The federal courts were also originally empowered with jurisdiction over problems airing between citizens of one state and the government of another state. The 11th amendment to the Constitution (ratified 1795) however removed from federal jurisdiction those cases in which citizens of one state were the plaintiffs and the government of another state was the defendant. The amendment, though, did not disturb the jurisdiction of the federal courts in cases in which a state government is a plaintiff and a citizen of another state the defendant. The federal courts also have exclusive jurisdiction in all patent and copyright cases and by congressional law in 1898, the federal courts were empowered with original jurisdiction in all bankruptcy cases.

The courts established under the powers granted by Article III Section 1 & 2 of the Constitution are known as Constitutional Courts. Judges of the Constitutional courts are appointed for life by the President with the approval of the Senate. These courts are the *district courts, lower courts of original jurisdiction,* **the courts of appeals** (before 1948, known as the circuit court of appeals), exercising appellate jurisdiction over the district courts and the *Supreme Court*. A district court functions in each of the more than ninety federal judicial districts and in the District of Columbia.

A court of appeals functions in each of the ten federal judicial circuits and also in the District of Columbia, (The federal district court and the circuit court of appeals of the District of Columbia performs all of the same functions discharged in the states by the state courts). All of the lower federal courts operate under the uniform rules of procedure promulgated by the Supreme Court.

The Supreme Court of the United States is the highest appellate court in the country and is a court of original jurisdiction according to the Constitution *"in all cases affecting ambassadors, other public ministers and consuls, and those in which a state shall be a party".* By virtue of its' power to declare legislation unconstitutional (see Section 1.2 Marbury vs. Madison), the Supreme Court is also the final arbitrator of all Constitutional questions.

Other federal courts, established by Congress under powers to be implied in other articles of the Constitution, are called legislative courts. These courts are the **Court of Claims, the Court of Customs and Patent Appeals, the Customs Court,** and the territorial courts established in the federally administered territories of the United States.

The special jurisdictions of these courts are defined by the Congress of the United States. (Except in the case of the territorial courts, which are courts of general jurisdiction), the specialized functions of these courts are suggested by their titles.

The State Courts - Each State has an independent system of courts operating under the laws and constitution of that particular individual state. Broadly speaking, the state courts are based on the English judicial system as it existed in colonial times, but as modified by succeeding statues. The character and names of the various courts differ from state to state, but the state courts as a whole have general jurisdiction, except in cases in which exclusive jurisdiction has by law been vested in the federal courts. In cases involving the United States Constitution or federal laws or treaties and the such, the state courts are governed by the decisions of the Supreme Court of the United States and their decisions are subject to review by it.

Cases involving the federal Constitution, federal laws, or treaties and the like, may be brought to either the state courts, or the federal courts. Ordinary **civil suits** not involving any of the aforementioned elements, can be brought only to the state courts, except in cases of different state citizenship between the parties, in which case the suit may be brought to a federal court. By an act of Congress, however, suits involving different federal questions, or different state citizenship may be brought to a federal court only when it is a civil suit that involves $3,000 or more. All such cases that involve a smaller amount must be brought to a state court only. In accordance with a congressional law, a suit brought before a state court may be removed to a federal court at the option of the defendant.

Bearing in mind that any statements about state courts that is trying to give a typical explanation of all of them is subject to many exceptions. The following may be taken as a general comprehensive statement of their respective jurisdictions, functions, and organization.

County courts of general original jurisdiction exercise both criminal and civil jurisdictions in most states. A few states maintain separate courts of criminal and civil law inherited from the English judicial system. Between the lower courts and the supreme appellate courts of each state in a number of states, are intermediate appellate courts which, like the federal courts of appeals, provide faster justice for individuals by disposing of a large number of cases which would otherwise be added to the overcrowded calendars of the higher courts. Courts of last resort, the highest appellate courts for the states in criminal and civil cases are usually called *State Supreme Courts*.

The state court system also includes a number of minor, local courts with limited jurisdictions; these courts dispose of minor offenses and relatively small civil actions. Included in this classification are police and municipal courts in various cities and towns, and the courts presided over by justices of the peace in rural areas.

Skill 9.2   Identifying basic civil liberties and civil rights guaranteed under the U.S. legal system

The terms "**civil liberties**" and "**civil rights**" are often used interchangeably, but there are some fine distinctions between the two terms. The term <u>civil liberties</u> is more often used to imply that the state has a positive role to play in assuring that all its' citizens will have equal protection and justice under the law with equal opportunities to exercise their privileges of citizenship and to participate fully in the life of the nation, regardless of race, religion, sex, color or creed. The term <u>civil rights</u> is used more often to refer to rights that may be described as guarantees that are specified as against the state authority implying limitations on the actions of the state to interfere with citizens' liberties. Although the term "civil rights" has thus been identified with the ideal of equality and the term "civil liberties" with the idea of freedom, the two concepts are really inseparable and interacting. Equality implies the proper ordering of liberty in a society so that one individual's freedom does not infringe on the rights of others.

The beginnings of civil liberties and the idea of civil rights in the United States go back to the ideas of the ancient Greeks. The experience of the early struggle for civil rights against the British and the very philosophies that led people to come to the New World in the first place were still fresh in people's minds. Religious freedom, political freedom, and the right to live one's life as one sees fit are basic to the American ideal. These were embodied in the ideas expressed in the Declaration of Independence and the Constitution.

All these ideas found their final expression in the United States Constitution's first ten amendments, known as the **Bill of Rights**. In 1789, the first Congress passed these first amendments and by December 1791, three-fourths of the states at that time had ratified them.   The Bill of Rights protects certain liberties and basic rights. James Madison who wrote the amendments said that the Bill of Rights does not give Americans these rights. People, Madison said, already have these rights. They are natural rights that belong to all human beings. The Bill of Rights simply prevents the governments from taking away these rights.

To summarize:

The first amendment guarantees the basic rights of freedom of religion, freedom of speech, freedom of the press, and freedom of assembly.

The next three amendments came out of the colonists' struggle with Great Britain. For example, the third amendment prevents Congress from forcing citizens to keep troops in their homes. Before the Revolution, Great Britain tried to coerce the colonists to house soldiers.

Amendments five through eight protect citizens who are accused of crimes and are brought to trial. Every citizen has the right to due process of law, (due process as defined earlier, being that the government must follow the same fair rules for everyone brought to trial.) These rules include the right to a trial by an impartial jury, the right to be defended by a lawyer, and the right to a speedy trial.

The last two amendments limit the powers of the federal government to those that are expressly granted in the Constitution, any rights not expressly mentioned in the Constitution, thus, belong to the states or to the people.

In regards to specific guarantees:

Freedom of Religion: Religious freedom has not been seriously threatened in the United States historically. The policy of the government has been guided by the premise that church and state should be separate. However, when religious practices have been at cross-purposes with attitudes prevailing in the nation at particular times, there has been restrictions placed on these practices. Some of these have been restrictions against the practice of polygamy that is supported by certain religious groups. The idea of animal sacrifice that is promoted by some religious beliefs is generally prohibited. The use of mind0altering illegal substances that some use in religious rituals has been restricted. In the United States, all recognized religious institutions are tax-exempt in following the idea of separation of church and state, and therefore, there have been many quasi-religious groups that have in the past tried to take advantage of this fact. All of these issues continue, and most likely will continue to occupy both political and legal considerations for some time to come.

Freedom of Speech, Press, and Assembly: These rights historically have been given wide latitude in their practices, though there has been instances when one or the other have been limited for various reasons. The classic limitation, for instance, in regards to freedom of speech, has been the famous precept that an individual is prohibited from yelling fire! in a crowded theatre. This prohibition is an example of the state saying that freedom of speech does not extend to speech that might endanger other people. There is also a prohibition against **slander,** or the knowingly stating of a deliberate falsehood against one party by another. There are many regulations regarding freedom of the press, the most common example are the various laws against **libel,** (or the printing of a known falsehood). In times of national emergency, various restrictions have been placed on the rights of press, speech and sometimes assembly.

The legal system in recent years has also undergone a number of serious changes, some would say challenges, with the interpretation of some constitutional guarantees.

America also has a number of organizations that present themselves as champions of the fight for civil liberties and civil rights in this country. Much criticism, however, has been raised at times against these groups as to whether or not they are really protecting rights, or following a specific ideology, perhaps attempting to create "new" rights, or in many cases, looking at the strict letter of the law, as opposed to what the law actually intends.

"Rights" come with a measure of responsibility and respect for the public order, all of which must be taken into consideration.

Overall, the American experience has been one of exemplary conduct in regards to the protection of individual rights. Where there has been a lag in its practice, notably the refusal to grant full and equal rights to blacks, the fact of their enslavement, and the second class status of women for much of American history, negates the good that the country has done in other areas. Other than the American Civil War, the country has proved itself to be more or less resilient in being able, for the most part, peacefully, to change when it has not lived up to its' stated ideals in practice. What has been called "the virtual bloodless civil rights revolution" is a case in point.

Though much effort and suffering accompanied the struggle, in the end it did succeed in changing the foundation of society in such a profound way that would have been unheard of in many other countries without the strong tradition of freedom and liberty that was, and is, the underlying feature of American society.

How best to move forward with ensuring civil liberties and civil rights for all continues to dominate the national debate. In recent times, issues seem to revolve not around individual rights but what has been called "group rights". At the forefront of the debate is whether some specific remedies like affirmative action, quotas, gerrymandering and various other forms of preferential treatment are actually fair or just as bad as the ills they are supposed to cure. At the present, no easy answers seem to be forthcoming. It is a testament to the American system that it has shown itself able to enter into these debates, to find solutions and tended to come out stronger.

The fact that the United States has the longest single constitutional history in the modern era is just one reason to be optimistic about the future of American liberty.

Competency 10.0   *Knowledge of citizenship*

Skill 10.1   **The process of acquiring citizenship and basic responsibilities of citizenship**

A citizen of the United States may either be native-born or a **naturalized** citizen. **Naturalization** is the process by which one acquires citizenship. Upon a specialized occasion, one may also have dual-citizenship, that is citizenship in the United States as well as in another country.

In order to become a citizen several involved requirements must first be met. Those necessary requirements for citizenship comprise eight specific steps and are as follows:

1. An individual applying for citizenship must be at least 18 years old.
2. The individual must have been lawfully admitted into the United States for permanent residence.
3. The individual must have lived in the United States on a continual basis for at least 5 years, not counting short trips outside the United States. In addition, one must have resided for at least six months in the state where one is going to file a petition for citizenship. (There are some important exceptions to this residency requirement. One exception is marriage to a spouse who is a citizen, which can shorten the residency requirement to 3 years. Other exceptions are made for certain spouses of citizens employed overseas and for alien members of the United States armed forces. Still other exceptions to the 5-year residency requirement apply to certain refugee groups under various specific federal laws on a case by case basis).
4. The individual must show a good moral character and believe in the principles of the Constitution of the United States of America.
5. The individual must not have been a member of the Communist Party for ten years prior to application for citizenship.
6. The individual must have not broken any immigration laws or to have been ordered to leave the United States.
7. The individual must be able to speak, understand, read and write simple English and must pass an examination about the history and government of the United States.
8. The individual must take an oath promising to give up foreign allegiance to obey the Constitution and laws of the United States and to fight for the United States of America, or do work of importance to the nation if asked lawfully to do so.

The entire naturalization process is accomplished in three separate steps. The first of which is the completion of the required application this is done only after an individual has met the previous eight requirements.

The "**Application to File Petition for Naturalization**", Form N-400, is used if an individual is applying for their own naturalization. The Immigration and Naturalization Service revises this form periodically, while they will accept the "older" application forms, it is important to obtain the latest one. The form itself consists of three parts, the application, Form N-400 itself, a fingerprint chart, and Form G-325, entitled *"Biographic Information"*. All applications must be properly filled out in order to be accepted. Once this is done and filed with the Immigration and Naturalization Service, it is reviewed, and if accepted, an individual will be so informed. They must then go to an appointed court to be officially sworn in by a judge or magistrate as a new citizen.

Once this is done, the individual is considered a citizen of the United States of America with all the privileges, rights and responsibilities that it entails. In addition to those rights that have previously been enumerated, the responsibilities include voting, jury duty, and the proper observance of the laws of the United States.

It is presumed that any citizen of the United States would recognize their responsibilities to the country and that the surest way of protecting their rights is by exercising those rights, which also entail a responsibility. Some examples include the *right* to vote and the *responsibility* to be well informed on various issues, the *right* to a trial by jury and the *responsibility* to ensure the proper working of the justice system by performing jury duty (rather than avoiding doing so). In the end, it is only by the mutual recognition of the fact that an individual has both rights and responsibilities in society that enables the society to function in order to protect those very rights.

Competency 11.0   Knowledge of international relations

Skill 11.1   Understanding the evolution of U.S. foreign policy

"Avoid European entanglements", these are the words spoken by George Washington in his famous farewell address upon leaving office after having served as the first President of the United States. This was meant to advise future American leaders that they should pursue an isolationist policy in regards to world, or European affairs. (Washington did approve of trade with other countries however).

The belief was that the old problems, conflicts, and squabbles of Europe were no place for the new nation to become involved in. Indeed, it was to escape these problems that people had come to the United States. That was why the United States was created.

This idea of separation has been the guiding policy of American foreign policy for most of its' history. Only in recent times has the United States even been willing to enter into any sort of treaties and mutual defense obligations with any other nation or nations.

While America did not want to get involved in European affairs, it also did not want the European powers involved in its' affairs, or the affairs of what it considered to be its' sphere of influence, namely the American hemisphere.

Thus, in 1803, President James Monroe would promulgate his famous **Monroe Doctrine**, which simply stated that the European powers should stay out of the American hemisphere, that only the United States would have any say in its development. It was saying to Europe, "you stay out of our affairs and we will stay out of yours".

This ideology has been strong against any European involvement in this hemisphere. Even with the growing American involvement in the rest of the world, the United States still says "stay out!" to any European power who would try to gain influence in this part of the world. Witness the American reactions to the communist revolutions in Cuba and Nicaragua. Also, the struggles of the United States against various revolutionary, insurgent movements in Central and South America, struggle seen as being against "foreign" powers and their ideologies, i.e. the former Soviet Union and the Communist Bloc.

In the years after the Revolution, American trade grew rapidly. Ships sailed out of New England ports on voyages that sometimes lasted three years or more. When the captains put into foreign ports, they kept a sharp lookout for trade goods and new markets in which to sell. Traders often took big risks, hoping for bigger profits in return. In 1784, the ship **Empress of China** became the first American ship to trade with China, before long American merchants had built up a profitable trade with China. American trading ships also ran great risks in the Mediterranean Sea. For many years, the rulers of the Barbary States on the coast of North Africa attacked American and European trading ships. The United States and many European countries were forced to pay a yearly tribute or bribe to protect their ships from attack. The ruler of Tripoli, one of the Barbary States, wanted the United States to pay an even larger tribute. The United States refused, coining the phrase "millions for defense, not one cent for tribute" (which actually sums up the foreign policy of the United States for all of its history). By 1805, America had managed to get the rulers of the Barbary Coast to stop harassing American shipping.

Events in Europe itself posed unexpected problems for the United States. In 1789, the **French Revolution** broke out. At first, most Americans supported the French Revolution. America knew what it meant to fight for liberty and France was America's first ally. Like many revolutions, the French Revolution soon however took a violent course. The French King, Louis XVI, and his family were imprisoned and executed. In the United States, opinion was divided. People like Hamilton was horrified at the Reign of Terror that swept France and killed thousands of people. Thomas Jefferson condemned the terror but thought that the violence was necessary for the French to win their freedom.

The French Revolution worried rulers and nobles all over Europe. They were afraid that revolutionary ideas would spread to their own lands. To prevent this, Great Britain, Austria, Prussia, The Netherlands, and Spain joined in a war against France. The fighting continued off and on from 1792 to 1815. The war in Europe also affected the United States. In 1778, the United States and France had signed a treaty of friendship. Under the treaty, France could use American ports. Now that France was at war with Britain, it wanted to use American ports to supply its ships and attack British ships. Washington's cabinet was divided over what course to follow. Alexander Hamilton argued that America's treaty with France was signed with King Louis XVI and since the king was dead the treaty was no longer in force. However, Thomas Jefferson favored the French cause. He was suspicious of Hamilton, who wanted friendly relations with Great Britain, America's old enemy.

Washington wanted to keep the United States out the European war in any case. Therefore, in April 1793, he issued the *Neutrality Proclamation.* It stated that the United States would not support either side in the war. It also forbade any American warlike action against either Great Britain or France. Despite the Neutrality Proclamation, problems arose because American merchants wanted to trade with both Great Britain and France. At the same time, each of these countries wanted to stop Americans from trading with its enemy.

In 1793, the British began attacking American ships that traded with the French colonies in the West Indies. Well-armed British warships chased and captured American merchant ships. When Americans learned of the British actions, many wanted to declare war. Washington, however, knew that the United States was in no position to fight a war. He sent Chief Justice **John Jay** to Britain for talks. After much hard bargaining, Jay worked out a treaty in 1794. The British agreed to pay damages for the ships taken in the West Indies, but they refused to make any promises about future attacks. Jay also wanted the British to give up the forts they still held on the American mainland in the Ohio Valley. The British agreed to do this only after the United States paid the debts it owed to British merchants since the Revolution. The Senate was unhappy with **Jay's Treaty**, but at Washington's urging, ratified it in 1795. Although the treaty was unpopular, Washington was satisfied that he had kept the United States out of war with Great Britain.

In 1803, the United States brought from France the vast area west of the Mississippi up to the Rocky Mountains in what was known as the Louisiana Purchase. This action more than doubled the size of the United States and gave America virtual control over the continent. This began an era of unprecedented growth and expansion for the United States both in population and in settlement. This expansion didn't end until it had settled all the land from the Atlantic Ocean to the Pacific Ocean and from the Canadian border to the Rio Grande. (In the process however it also wiped out the remains of the indigenous Indian populations to almost non-existence).

During the early 1800s, America faced another problem on the high seas. In 1803, Great Britain, with a coalition of other European powers, went to war against France and the power of Napoleon Bonaparte in Europe. At first, America profited from the war. British and French ships were so busy fighting that they could not engage in trade. American merchants took advantage of the war to trade with both sides. As trade increased, American shipbuilders hurried to build new ships. However, Great Britain and France each tried to cut off trade to the other country. Americans claimed that they were neutral, but the warring countries ignored this claim. Napoleon seized American ships bound for England. At the same time, the British seized American ships carrying goods to and from France.

Between 1805 and 1807, hundreds of American ships were seized. Not only did Great Britain seize American ships, however, but it also took American sailors and seaman and forced them to serve on British ships. This practice was called **Impressment**. Because of the war with France, the British navy needed all the sailors it could find. Its warships began stopping and searching American merchant ships and impressing American sailors. Americans were furious with the British for impressing their sailors and attacking their ships. Many Americans, known as **War Hawks**, wanted to declare war on Britain. The then President, Thomas Jefferson wanted to avoid war. He knew that the small American Navy could not match the powerful British fleet.

Instead in 1807, he convinced Congress to pass the *Embargo Act*. The Embargo Act forbade Americans to export or import any goods. Jefferson hoped that the embargo would hurt Britain and France because they would be unable to get badly needed goods. He would offer to end the embargo if they would let Americans trade in peace. The embargo hurt the Europeans but it hurt Americans as well. So in 1809, Congress repealed the Embargo Acts and replaced it with the **Non-Intercourse Act**. Under this Act, Americans could trade with all nations except Britain and France. If these nations agreed to stop seizing American ships and sailors, trade could resume with them as well.

James Madison became President in 1809. He hoped that Britain and France would give in to American pressure. In 1810, Napoleon in France promised to respect the rights of America ships, so Madison let American ships trade with France. The British refused to make a similar promise so the embargo against Great Britain continued.

The War Hawks kept up their pressure for war. They had good arguments, which were that the United States must defend its rights at sea and end impressment. They urged Americans to conquer Canada and seize Florida, which at that time still belonged to Spain, Great Britain's ally.

Finally, in June of 1812, President Madison asked Congress to declare war on Great Britain. The Congress quickly acted and the *War of 1812* had begun. The United States was not ready for war, however. The American army was small and poorly trained; its navy had only 16 ships fit to fight against the huge British navy. Yet during the war, American ships won several victories at sea, (though in the end these did very little to affect the outcome of the war). In 1812, the War Hawks demanded an invasion of Canada. They expected the Canadians to welcome them and the chance to throw off British rule. However, the Canadians did not welcome America and fought back forcing America to retreat and give up any ideas of conquering Canada. In 1814, Great Britain and its' allies defeated Napoleon and France in Europe. The British then began sending its best troops to invade America.

In August 1814, British troops invaded Washington, DC burning what was then called the President's Mansion. It was later fixed and repainted white, hence, its' present name). Then the British marched north to Baltimore where they were defeated and forced to withdraw. Francis Scott Key wrote the Star Spangled Banner at this time to commemorate the battle and the American victory. Peace negotiations began late in 1814 and in December 1814, the *Treaty of Ghent* was signed in Belgium officially ending the war.

In the end, very little was actually settled. For instance, the treaty said nothing about impressment or the right of neutrals. Each side agreed to go back to prewar conditions.

The United States learned several important lessons from the war, namely the need to keep and maintain a strong navy and a strong and well-trained army. Little by little, it was finding itself involved in world affairs and would thus have to adjust its thinking accordingly. Although Spain lost many of its' colonies in America by the early 1800s it still held on to Puerto Rico, Cuba, and Florida. Americans thought that Florida should be added to the United States. As early as 1810, President Madison had claimed West Florida, the area of land over the Gulf of Mexico. Concern over the Spanish in Florida grew, especially among Southerners. Slaves from Georgia and other southern states often fled into Florida. In addition, Indians from Florida sometimes launched raids from Florida against Americans in Georgia. The Spanish did little to stop these raids.

In 1818, President Monroe launched an attack against the Indians in Florida. This angered the Spanish. However, because Spain was already fighting rebels in Mexico and elsewhere at this time, it did not want war with the United States. **John Quincy Adams**, son of the second President of the United States, was President Monroe's Secretary of State. Adams worked out a treaty with Spain that went into effect in 1821. In the *Adams-Onis Treaty*, Spain gave Florida to the United States in return for a payment of $5 million.

Throughout these years, America continued to grow and to prosper. Mostly now, it began to look inward and westward. Horace Greeley, the writer, had told people to "go West", and they did so to an unusual extent. They traveled all the way to the coast of California and began developing and settling the land. America was confident at this time and Americans felt their democratic government was the best in the world. Many Americans felt it was their right and their duty to expand and to control all the land from coast to coast. By the 1840s, the phrase *Manifest Destiny* appeared. It came to mean that the Americans had a clear and obvious "manifest" destiny to expand all the way to the Pacific Ocean regardless of what they had to do to achieve it.

In 1821, Mexico gained its own independence from Spain. It allowed Americans to settle in the area of Texas. The newly independent Mexican government thought that the Americans would help to develop the land. It also hoped that the settlers would help it against the Indians still living there. However, as more and more settlers arrived, problems arose between the Americans and the Mexican authorities. In 1830, the government of Mexico forbade any more American settlers from moving to Texas. By October 1835, fighting had broken out between the settlers and the Mexican army. The settlers managed to do well against the Mexican army. On March 2, 1836, the Americans in Texas declared themselves independent as the Republic of Texas. It was at the same time that the famous battle between the American settlers and the Mexican army took place at the San Antonio mission known as *The Alamo*. The slaughter of the Americans at the Alamo both angered and inspired the Texans. It also brought in a flood of volunteers into the Texan army from the United States itself.

On April 21, 1836 after the Mexican defeat at the battle of **San Jacinto**, the Texans won their independence. In the United States, feelings were divided about whether or not the country should annex Texas. By 1844, Americans had come to believe that annexing Texas would be in their best interests. The nation was expanding quickly and it seemed only natural that Texas should become part of the nation. Thus in March 1845, Texas officially became part of the Union. Problems over the Texas border with Mexico would continue to remain however.

At the same time as the events over Texas were taking place, problems arising with Great Britain over its remaining land holdings on the continent were coming to a head. These mostly involved the area of Oregon and the border with Canada. Though America and Great Britain nearly went to war, a compromise was worked out. The border was divided at the line of the 49th N. Latitude. The area north went to Canada. The area south went to the United States as the Oregon Territory. It was then divided into three states. Oregon became a state in 1859, Washington in 1889, and Idaho in 1890.

Problems with Mexico however were not so easily solved. The United States and Mexico stood at the brink of war in 1845. The Mexicans were furious when the United States annexed Texas. They had never accepted the independence of Texas, also they were afraid that Americans living in the areas of what is now California and New Mexico might rebel as they had done in Texas. Americans in turn were angry with Mexico as well. President Polk, who was in office at that time, offered to buy California and New Mexico from Mexico, but they refused. Many Americans felt that the Mexicans were standing in the way of their Manifest Destiny. The **Mexican War** finally broke out in 1846.

In 1847, the Americans won the war and the *Treaty of Hidalgo* was signed in 1848. America gained California and New Mexico in what was called the **Mexican Cession**. The Mexican-Texas border was established at the Rio Grande River in southern Texas. In return, the United States agreed to pay Mexico $15 million and to respect the rights of Spanish speakers in the territories now under their control. A few years after the Mexican War, the United States completed its expansion across the continent. In 1853, it paid Mexico $10 million for a strip of land now in Arizona and New Mexico. The land was called the **Gadsden Purchase**. America had now completed its goal of Manifest Destiny.

However, divisions in the country began to appear over what its future form was to be. They involved for the most part the question of states rights and the issue of slavery. The northern part of the country was generally very well industrialized and non-slave holding with a strong support for the federal Union. The southern areas were more agricultural, slave-owning and with a strong belief in the idea of states' rights. The situation deteriorated steadily throughout the middle of the 1800s, and in 1860, finally erupted into a full-scale civil war. This situation also led for a while to the establishment of two separate and distinct foreign policies. The north, known as the Union, wanted the other powers, namely the Europeans to say out of the war. While the south known as the Confederacy, wanted European involvement to help them win their independence from the north, the south had strong trade relations with many European countries. However, in the end, the north proved stronger and the European powers were unable to influence the course of the war in any real or meaningful way. This was in no small measure one of the reasons that the north managed to win the war by 1865.

After the Civil War ended, increased trade created new links between the United States and other countries. By then, the United States was producing more food and manufactured goods than it needed, so Americans began exporting goods to foreign nations at a ever increasing rate. Europe, ironically, was still the most important market. However, trade with China, Japan, Korea, and the emerging countries of Central and South America grew as well. At the same time that the United States was increasing its trade, the European countries were also building up their empires in Africa and Asia. As these empires grew and increased the power and wealth of the European nations, Americans began to fear that they would be squeezed out of many of the new, emerging, foreign markets.

In 1867, the United States bought Alaska from Russia. Originally called "**Seward's Folly**", after the then Secretary of State, Alaska was almost forgotten. Then in 1896, gold was discovered in the Klondike region. This helped to open Alaska up for settlement. In the end, the Alaska purchase turned out to be a very good bargain and an important asset as the land is full of various mineral resources and petroleum. In the 1890s, the United States would gain territory overseas. For instance, in 1898 it annexed Hawaii. It had good harbors for the growing American fleet. From there, trading ships and navy ships could sail to Asia and the Far East. This meant that the United States could then open and protect new markets in this region.

The **Spanish-American War of 1898** also gave the United States new territories. The war broke out because of disputes arising over Spanish actions in Cuba. American troops quickly defeated the Spanish forces and under the peace treaty the islands of Puerto Rico in the Caribbean, and Guam and the Philippines in the Pacific, became territories belonging to the United States. Cuba itself became an independent nation.

In 1901, Theodore Roosevelt became President. His motto was *"speak softly and carry a big stick"*. By this he meant that the United States would strive for peace but not shy away from using force when it felt it was necessary. Roosevelt used the "big stick" in Latin America. Several European countries were trying to influence the course of events in countries like Venezuela and the Dominican Republic. Roosevelt reminded them that the Monroe Doctrine forbade "foreign" nations from meddling in this region.

In 1903, the United States built a canal in the area of the Isthmus of Panama and came to control an area known as the ***Panama Canal Zone***. Panama itself became an independent country thanks to American intervention. It had been a part of Columbia before this. Throughout the period of the 1900's, the United States intervened several more times in the countries of Central and South America. This was done whenever various Presidents felt it necessary to do so in order to protect what they perceived as vital American interests.

For instance, President Taft sent troops into Nicaragua and Honduras. President Wilson sent marines to the island of Haiti and in 1984, President Reagan ordered American troops to invade the island of Grenada in order to protect American students and civilians who had been living there.

In the Far East, with the outbreak of the *Russo-Japanese* War in the beginning of 1905, Theodore Roosevelt took an active role. He secured from the belligerents the right of neutrality for all of China, except for the disputed area of Manchuria. He was also instrumental in arranging a peace treaty, the **Treaty of Portsmouth**, which ended the war by the end of 1905. Relations with the rest of the world were also generally smooth at this time. There were conflicts over the rights of ships to use the Panama Canal, protests by Japan over the treatment of Japanese in the United States because at the time Japanese could not legally own land, and a growing conflict with Mexico which would erupt into open violence in 1916.

In 1914, World War I broke out in Europe. At first, President Wilson kept the United States neutral. President Wilson's wishes were not sufficient however to prevent strong pro-British feelings from arising. American sentiment especially turned angry over several serious violations of American neutrality, violations committed by both sides in fact, but mostly by Germany. The sinking of the steamship **Lusitania** in May 1915 by the Germans is the most notorious.

In 1917, America entered the war on the side of Great Britain and its allies versus Germany and its allies. American involvement came none too soon. At this time, the triumph of the *Bolshevik* (Communist) Party led by Vladimir Lenin in the Russian Revolution caused Russia to leave the war. Germany was able now to bring its full force against the Western allies of Britain and France.

When peace came the next year with the surrender of Germany and its allies, many Americans wanted to return to the policy of staying out of world affairs. They were called *isolationists*. This fact was instrumental in the United States staying out of what was President's Wilson's brainchild, an organization set up to work for world peace, **The League of Nations**. Without American involvement, the organization proved to be ineffective in stopping aggression and ultimately in preventing the Second World War.

The First World War also had unintended consequences. As mentioned, it led in 1917 to the rise of power of Communism in Russia and to the creation of the Soviet Union. An event which would come to dominate American foreign policy for the next 70 years.

By the 1930s, after a period of strong economic growth, the United States as well as the rest of the world, entered a period of economic decline known as the Depression. The new American President, Franklin Roosevelt, as well as the country as a whole were more concerned initially with domestic affairs. Roosevelt thus tried to pursue peace and cooperation, especially in regards to the American continent and the nations of Central and South America. His policy was called the "**Good Neighbor Policy**". However, in Europe matters were becoming more difficult because the worldwide economic downturn had more serious effects.

Because of the problems in Europe, the isolationist mood in the United States continued with ever increasing support well into the late 1930s. With the rise to power of dictatorships in Germany and Italy the general trend toward war in the 1930s progressed. Many in the United States, most notably President Franklin Roosevelt, came to see that it was in America's interest to promote peace and democracy in the world. A country as big and as powerful as the United States could not realistically continue to remove itself from world affairs. Nevertheless, since the general mood in the nation at that time was away from world involvement and in favor of isolation, not much could be done internationally. Memories of the slaughter of the First World War were too strong for many to even consider getting involved in another European conflict. George Washington's warning against "entangling alliances in the problems and conflicts of Europe" was very much in mind.

After the outbreak of war in 1939, the American government had to proclaim a public stance of neutrality. While covertly and carefully doing what it could to aid its friends and allies. This involved the process that came to be known as **Lend-Lease**, in which the United States would give, on what was presumed a temporary basis, certain war supplies to the forces fighting Germany and its' allies. This helped them to maintain themselves during Nazi Germany's attacks. At first, Lend-Lease went only to Great Britain. When Germany attacked the Soviet Union in June 1941, it went there as well.

The American isolationist mood was given a shocking and lasting blow in 1941 with the Japanese attack on Pearl Harbor. The nation arose and forcefully entered the international arena as never before. Declaring itself "the arsenal of democracy", it entered the Second World War and emerged not only victorious, but also as the *strongest power* on the Earth. It would now, like it or not, have a permanent and leading place in world affairs.

Since the end of the Second World War, the United States has perceived its greatest threat to be the expansion of Communism in the world. To that end, it has devoted a larger and larger share of its foreign policy, diplomacy, and both economic and military might to combating it.

In the aftermath of the Second World War, with the Soviet Union having emerged as the *second* strongest power on Earth, the United States embarked on a policy known as "**Containment**" of the Communist menace. This involved what came to be known as the "**Marshall Plan**" and the "**Truman Doctrine**". The Marshall Plan involved the economic aid that was sent to Europe in the aftermath of the Second World War aimed at preventing the spread of communism.

The Truman Doctrine offered military aid to those countries that were in danger of communist upheaval. This led to the era known as the **Cold War** in which the United States took the lead along with the Western European nations against the Soviet Union and the Eastern Bloc countries. It was also at this time that the United States finally gave up on George Washington's' advice against "European entanglements" and joined the **North Atlantic Treaty Organization** or **NATO**. This was formed in 1949 and was comprised of the United States and several Western European nations for the purposes of opposing communist aggression.

The **United Nations** was also formed at this time (1945) to replace the defunct League of Nations for the purposes of ensuring world peace. Even with American involvement, would prove largely ineffective in maintaining world peace.

In the 1950s, the United States embarked on what was called the "**Eisenhower Doctrine**", after the then President Eisenhower. This aimed at trying to maintain peace in a troubled area of the world, the Middle East. However, unlike the Truman Doctrine in Europe, it would have little success.

The United States also became involved in a number of world conflicts in the ensuing years. Each had at the core the struggle against communist expansion. Among these were the **Korean War** (1950-1953), the **Vietnam War** (1965-1975), and various continuing entanglement in Central and South America and the Middle East. By the early 1970's under the leadership of then Secretary of State, Henry Kissinger, the United States and its allies embarked on the policy that came to be known as "**Détente**". This was aimed at the easing of tensions between the United States and its allies and the Soviet Union and its allies.

By the 1980s, the United States embarked on what some saw as a renewal of the Cold War. This owed to the fact that the United States was becoming more involved in trying to prevent communist insurgency in Central America. A massive expansion of its armed forces and the development of space-based weapons systems were undertaken at this time. As this occurred, the Soviet Union, with a failing economic system and a foolhardy adventure in Afghanistan, found itself unable to compete. By 1989, events had come to a head. This ended with the breakdown of the Communist Bloc, the virtual end of the monolithic Soviet Union, and the collapse of the communist system by the early 1990's.

Now the United States remains active in world affairs in trying to promote peace and reconciliation, with a new specter rising to challenge it and the world, the specter of nationalism.

SAMPLE TEST

DIRECTIONS: Read each item and select the best response.

1. The term that best describes how the Supreme Court can block laws that may be unconstitutional from being enacted is:

   A. Jurisprudence

   B. Judicial Review

   C. Exclusionary Rule

   D. Right Of Petition

2. On the spectrum of American politics the label that most accurately describes voters to the "right of center" is:

   A. Moderates

   B. Liberals

   C. Conservatives

   D. Socialists

3. Marxism believes which two groups are in continual conflict?

   A. Farmers and landowners

   B. Kings and the nobility.

   C. Workers and owners

   D. Structure and superstructure

4. The United States legislature is bi-cameral, this means:

   A. It consists of several houses

   B. It consists of two houses

   C. The Vice-President is in charge of the legislature when in session.

   D. It has an upper house and a lower house

5. What Supreme Court ruling established the principal of Judicial Review?

   A. Jefferson vs. Madison

   B. Lincoln vs. Douglas

   C. Marbury vs. Madison

   D. Marbury vs. Jefferson

6. To be eligible to be elected President one must:

   A. Be a citizen for at least five years

   B. Be a citizen for seven years

   C. Have been born a citizen

   D. Be a naturalized citizen

7. **The international organization established to work for world peace at the end of Second World War is the:**

   A. League of Nations

   B. United Federation of Nations

   C. United Nations

   D. United World League

8. **In the United States, the right to declare war is a power of:**

   A. The President

   B. Congress

   C. The Executive Branch

   D. The States

9. **Which of the following is a example of a direct democracy?**

   A. Elected representatives

   B. Greek city-states

   C. The United States Senate

   D. The United States House of Representatives

10. **To plead "the Fifth Amendment" means to:**

    A. Refuse to speak so one does not incriminate oneself

    B. Plead "no contest" in court

    C. Ask for freedom of speech

    D. Ask to appear before a judge when charged with a crime

11. **The founder of the first Communist party and the first leader of the Soviet Union was:**

    A. Joseph Stalin

    B. Vladimir Lenin

    C. John Lennon

    D. Karl Marx

12. **The political document that was the first to try to organize the newly *independent* American Colonies was the:**

    A. Declaration of Independence

    B. Articles of Confederation

    C. The Constitution

    D. The Confederate States

13. The first organized city-states arose in:

   A. Egypt

   B. China

   C. Sumer

   D. Greece

14. In Florida the city government type gaining widespread acceptance because of its greater efficiency is the:

   A. Mayor-council

   B. Council-manager

   C. Civil commission

   D. Town meeting

15. The founder of the first Communist Party and the first leader of the Soviet Union was:

   A. Joseph Stalin

   B. Vladimir Lenin

   C. John Lennon

   D. Karl Marx

16. The first ten amendments to the Constitution are called:

   A. Bill of Petition

   B. Petition of Rights

   C. Rights of Man

   D. Bill of Rights

17. Socialists believe that the government should have a _____ role in the economy:

   A. Lesser

   B. Greater

   C. Equal with business

   D. Less than business

18. One difference between *totalitarianism* and *authoritarianism* is that totalitarianism believes in:

   A. Total control over all aspects of society

   B. Minimum government control

   C. There is no difference

   D. The difference is unknown

19. The constitution is called a "living document" because:

    A. It has the ability to change with different times ⁀

    B. It was created by people

    C. It is a static document

    D. Excessive reliance on the Constitution will kill it

20. In the feudal system who has the most power?

    A. The peasant or serf

    B. The noble or lord ⁀

    C. The worker

    D. The merchant

21. The idea that the European powers should stay out of the affairs of the American hemisphere is known as:

    A. Containment policy

    B. The Eisenhower Doctrine

    C. Neo-isolationism

    D. The Monroe Doctrine ⁀

22. In Marxism another name for the workers is the:

    A. Proletariat ⁀

    B. Peasants

    C. Bourgeoisie

    D. Protester

23. Fascism first arose in:

    A. Austria

    B. Germany

    C. Italy ⁀

    D. Russia

24. The Exclusionary Rule prevents:

    A. Illegally seized evidence from being used in court ⁀

    B. Persons from incriminating themselves in court

    C. Police from entering a private home for any reason

    D. Any evidence however gathered from being used in court if it is objected to by one side in a court case

25. **The idea that "the government is best that governs least" is most closely associated with:**

    A. The Soviet Communist system

    B. The American Free Enterprise system

    C. British Conservatism

    D. Mussolini's Corporate State

26. **In the United States Constitution political parties are:**

    A. Never actually mentioned

    B. Called "a necessary part of the political process".

    C. Most effective if they are only two major ones

    D. Called harmful to the political process

27. **Civil suits deal mostly with, but not totally with:**

    A. Money

    B. Violent crime

    C. The government

    D. Not given

28. **"Common law" refers mostly to:**

    A. The precedents and traditions that have gone before in society so that they become accepted norms.

    B. The laws dealing with the "common people"

    C. Law that is written and codified

    D. The House of Commons in Great Britain

29. **Anarchists believe in:**

    A. Strong government

    B. Corporate state system

    C. Weak, mild government

    D. No government

30. The U.S. government's federal system consists of:

A. Three parts, the Executive, the Legislative, and the Judiciary

B. Three parts, the Legislative, the Congress, and the Presidency

C. Four parts, the Executive, the Judiciary, the courts, and the Legislative

D. Two parts, the Government, and the governed

31. One difference between a presidential and a parliamentary system is that in a parliamentary system :

A. The Prime Minister is head of government, while a president or monarch is head of state.

B. The President is head of government, and the Vice-President is head of state

C. The President pro-tempore of the senate is head of state while the prime minister is head of government.

D. The President appoints the head of state

32. The American concept of Manifest Destiny means:

A. America had a right to spread throughout the American continent from coast to coast.

B. The United States should respect the right of native peoples it encounters in its push westward.

C. The rest of the world powers should stay out of this part of the world

D. America should strive to be the dominant world power

33. In an <u>indirect</u> democracy:

A. All the people together decide on issues

B. People elect representatives to act for them

C. Democracy can never really work

D. Government is less efficient than a direct democracy

34. In a communist system _____ controls the means of production:

   A. A professional managerial class

   B. The owners of business and industry

   C. The workers

   D. The state

35. The Congress can override a presidents veto with a _____ vote:

   A. One-half

   B. Two-thirds

   C. Six-tenths

   D. Three-fourths

36. To become a citizen a individual must generally have lived in the United States for at least:

   A. Six years

   B. Five years

   C. One year

   D. Ten years

37. Give the correct order of the following:

   A. The Constitution, the Declaration of Independence, the Articles of Confederation

   B. The Declaration of Independence, the Constitution, the Articles of Confederation

   C. The Declaration of Independence, the Articles of Confederation, the Constitution

   D. The Articles of Confederation, the Declaration of Independence, the Constitution.

38. The ability of the President to veto an act of Congress is an example of:

   A. Separation of Powers

   B. Checks and Balances

   C. Judicial Review

   D. Presidential Perogative

39. To "impeach" a President means to:

A. Bring charges against a president

B. Remove a president from office

C. Re-elect the president

D. Override his veto

40. An obligation identified with citizenship is:

A. Belonging to a political party

B. Educating oneself

C. Running for political office

D. Voting

41. The doctrine that sought to keep communism from spreading was:

A. The Cold War

B. Roll-back

C. Containment

D. Detente

42. The power to declare war, establish a postal system, and coin money rests with which branch of the government:

A. Presidential

B. Judicial

C. Legislative

D. Executive

43. If a president neither signs nor vetoes a bill officially for ten days it is called:

A. A pocket veto

B. A refused law

C. Unconstitutional to do that

D. A presidential veto

44. What was George Washington's advice to Americans about foreign policy?

A. America should have strong alliances

B. America should avoid alliances

C. Foreign policy should take precedence over domestic policy

D. Domestic policy should take precedence over foreign policy

45. How did the United States gain Florida from Spain?

A. It was captured from Spain after the Spanish American War

B. It was given to the British and became part of the original thirteen colonies

C. America bought it from Spain

D. America acquired it after the First World War

46. The belief that Government should stay out of economic affairs is called:

A. Mercantilism

B. Laissez-faire

C. Democratic-Socialism

D. Corporatism

47. The term that describes the division of government function is:

A. Free Enterprise

B. Constitutional Prerogative

C. Checks and Balances

D. Separation of Powers

48. Which of the following is an important idea expressed in the Declaration of Independence:

A. People have the right to change their government

B. People should obey the government authority

C. A monarchy is a bad thing

D. Indirect democracy is best

49. Florida has pioneered what innovative form of local government?

A. Metropolitan Government

B. Limited Government

C. Mayor-Council system

D. County-Commission system

50. Machiavelli was most concerned with describing:

A. Modern warfare

B. Ancient political philosophy

C. Representative government

D. Getting and keeping political power

51. Oligarchy refers to:

A. Rule of a single leader

B. The rule of a single political party

C. Rule by a select few

D. Rule by many

52. The Judiciary Act of 1789 established the:

A. Supreme Court

B. Principle of Judicial Review

C. State court system

D. Federal and circuit court system

53. The international organization established to work for world peace at the end of the First World War was the:

A. United Earth League

B. Confederate States

C. United Nation

D. League of Nations

54. Which statement closely resembles the political philosophy of John Hobbes?

A. Citizens should give unquestioning obedience to the state authority so long as it can maintain public order

B. That citizens have a right to rise against the state whenever they choose

C. All state authority is basically evil and should be eliminated

D. People are generally good and cooperative if given a chance

55. As a rule, the relationship between fascism and communism is:

A. They are the same thing

B. Unknown at present

C. Antagonistic

D. Cooperative

56. In the United States, the right to declare war is a power of:

A. The President

B. Congress

C. The Executive

D. The States

57. To plead "the Fifth Admendment", means to:

A. Refuse to speak so one does not incriminate oneself

B. Plead "no contest" in court

C. Ask for freedom of speech

D. Ask to appear before a judge when charged with a crime

58. A "tort" refers to:

A. A private or civil action brought into court

B. A type of confection

C. A penal offense

D. One who solicits

59. A boycott is:

A. The refusal to buy goods or services

B. An imbalance of trade

C. The refusal to speak in court

D. A Writ of Assistance

60. In the United States checks and balances refers to:

A. The ability of each branch of government to "check" or limit the actions of the others

B. Balance of payments

C. International law

D. The federal deficit

61. An amendment is:

A. A change or addition to the United States Constitution

B. The right of a state to secede from the Union

C. To add a state to the Union

D. The right of the Supreme Court to check actions of Congress and the President

62. The Executive branch refers to:

A. The Senate

B. The Legislature

C. Congress

D. The President and Vice-President

63. An "Ex Post facto Law" is:

A. A law made against an act after it has been committed

B. A law proclaimed unconstitutional by the Supreme Court

C. An Executive Act

D. A law relating to the postal system

64. The Judiciary refers to:

A. The President

B. Congress

C. The legal system

D. The system of states' rights

65. A tariff is:

A. A law passed by the Congress and vetoed by the President

B. An appointed official mandated to preserve public order

C. A tax a government places on internationally traded goods, usually goods entering a country

D. A tax a government places on goods produced for domestic use, another name for it is a "sales tax"

66. Maps as a rule are:

A. All subject to some sort of distortion

B. Always entirely accurate

C. Not very useful in political science studies

D. Difficult usually to understand

67. In a parliamentary system the person who becomes Prime Minister is usually:

A. The leader of the majority party in the legislature

B. Elected by a direct national vote

C. Chosen by the president of the country

D. Chosen by the cabinet

68. The Declaration of Independence owes much to the philosophy of:

A. Vladimir Lenin

B. Karl Marx

C. Thomas Hobbes

D. John Locke

69. **Florida was originally settled by:**

    A. Italy

    B. Great Britain

    C. Spain

    D. France

70. **The "cult of the personality" is an idea most associated with:**

    A. Democracy

    B. Anarchism

    C. Fascism

    D. Communism

71. **The highest appellate court in the United States is the:**

    A. National Appeals Court

    B. Circuit Court

    C. Supreme Court

    D. Court of Appeals

72. **The State of Florida has _____ counties:**

    A. 16

    B. 12

    C. 67

    D. 42

73. **The Bill of Rights was mostly written by:**

    A. Thomas Jefferson

    B. James Madison

    C. George Washington

    D. Alexander Hamilton

74. **The U.S. Constitution was ratified by the required number of states in:**

    A. August, 1861

    B. July, 1776

    C. June, 1788

    D. September, 1848

75. **To be a *naturalized* citizen means:**

    A. To have been refused citizenship

    B. To have dual-citizenship

    C. To be a "natural", or native born citizen

    D. To acquire citizenship

76. George Washington's opinion of America having trade with other nations was:

   A. Approval in only some instances

   B. Disapproval

   C. Approval

   D. Unsure

77. The "history of all societies is one of class struggle"' is a statement associated with:

   A. John Locke

   B. Thomas Jefferson

   C. Karl Marx

   D. Thomas Hobbes

78. "Walk softly and carry a big stick" is a statement associated with:

   A. Franklin Roosevelt

   B. Theodore Roosevelt

   C. George Washington

   D. Thomas Hobbes

79. Florida has been _____ in local government reform:

   A. A leader

   B. Following

   C. Unsure

   D. Unwilling to change

80. The Bill of Rights says that any rights it does not mention are:

   A. Reserved to the federal government

   B. Not important

   C. Judged by the Supreme Court

   D. Reserved to the states or to the people

81. Florida first became a state in:

   A. 1778

   B. 1845

   C. 1513

   D. 1868

82. The name for those who make maps is:

   A.   Haberdasher

   B.   Geographer

   C.   Cartographer

   D.   Demographer

83. An important aspect of statistics is:

   A.   The rate of proportional increase

   B.   The rate of increase

   C.   Tests of redundancy

   D.   Tests of reliability

84. The process of the state taking over industries and businesses is called:

   A.   Industrialization

   B.   Nationalization

   C.   Redistribution

   D.   Amalgamation

85. The first permanent settlement in Florida was:

   A.   St. Marcus

   B.   Fort Caroline

   C.   St. Helena

   D.   St. Augustine

86. The first election in which political parties played a role was in :

   A.   1787

   B.   1776

   C.   1888

   D.   1796

87. The vast land area west of the Mississippi River that the United States bought from France was:

   A.   California and New Mexico

   B.   The State of Florida

   C.   The Louisiana Purchase

   D.   The Gadsden Purchase

88. **The act of hijacking sailors on the high seas was called:**

    A. Internment

    B. Interaction

    C. Interrogation

    D. Impressment

89. **The War of 1812 involved the United States and:**

    A. Russia

    B. Great Britain

    C. France

    D. Spain

90. **The term "*suffrage*" means:**

    A. The right to vote

    B. The power of the court

    C. A Supreme Court ruling

    D. Legislative action

91. **What was "Seward's Folly"?**

    A. The purchase of Alaska

    B. The purchase of Louisiana

    C. The Mexican-American War

    D. The annexation of Texas

92. **Those who wanted the United States to stay out of world affairs were called:**

    A. Neo-Conservatives

    B. Isolationists

    C. Non-Interventionists

    D. Nationalists

93. **The early ancient civilizations developed systems of government:**

    A. To provide for defense against attack

    B. To regulate trade

    C. To regulate and direct the economic activities of the people as they worked together in groups

    D. To decide on the boundaries of the different fields during planting seasons

94. The process of putting the features of the earth on a flat surface is called:

A.   Presentation

B.   Projection

C.   Condensation

D.   Mercatorization

95. Florida was discovered by:

A.   Ponce de Leon

B.   Fernando Cortes

C.   Francisco Balboa

D.   Christopher Columbus

96. The most common type of local government in the United States at present is:

A.   Commission-Manager

B.   President-Legislature

C.   Council-Manager

D.   Mayor-Council

97. The first political parties in the United States were:

A.   Democratic-Republicans and Nationalists

B.   Progressives and Populists

C.   Democratic-Republicans and Federalists

D.   Democrats and Republicans

98. To become a citizen one must be at least _____ old:

A.   25 years

B.   18 years

C.   21 years

D.   19 years

99. The Spanish-American War started in:

A.   1889

B.   1914

C.   1927

D.   1898

100. A major feature of many multi-party political systems is:

A.   Separation of powers

B.   Inability to represent sectional interests

C.   Coalition government —

D.   Strong centralized government

101. Which of the following statements about American history is an opinion rather than a fact?

A.   The doctrine of Manifest Destiny can be said to have been an excuse for the expansionism of the United States on the American continent

B.   America's wealth, power, and influence increased with its size

C.   America's expansion was justified by its superior political and economic system

D.   The expansion of the United States was generally detrimental to the interests of native peoples

102. Which is a shared power of the federal and state governments?

A.   The power to declare war

B.   The power to build roads —

C.   The power to coin money

D.   The power to regulate interstate trade

103. The foreign policy known as the "Good Neighbor Policy" was associated with the administration of:

A.   James Madison

B.   Franklin Roosevelt

C.   Woodrow Wilson

D.   Theodore Roosevelt —

104. Direct democracy was a feature of:

A.   The politics of the Greek city-states —

B.   Ancient Rome

C.   Medieval Europe

D.   Sumerian Theocracy

105. In a Constitutional Monarchy, like that of Great Britain, that has a parliamentary system of government the sovereign takes the place of the:

   A. Prime Minister

   B. President

   C. Premier

   D. The Speaker of Parliament

106. The first constitution of Florida when it rejoined the Union after the Civil War was adopted in:

   A. 1868

   B. 1845

   C. 1865

   D. 1877

107. The type of city administration that is supposed to eliminate political patronage and fiscal waste is:

   A. Commission-Council

   B. Mayor-Council

   C. Council-Manager

   D. Metropolitan-Manager

108. Which of the following statements about the Supreme Court is true?

   A. "The Supreme Court has only an appellate jurisdiction in all matters".

   B. "The Supreme Court shall have original jurisdiction in all areas involving foreign officials, public officials, and cases in which a state is a party".

   C. "The Supreme Court shall exercise original jurisdiction only over those cases involving the Chief Executive".

   D. "The Supreme Court shall have original jurisdiction over appellate matters only".

109. "Man was born free and everywhere he is in chains", is a statement associated with:

   A. Thomas Jefferson

   B. John Locke

   C. Jean-Jacques Rousseau

   D. Karl Marx

110. **What happens if the President vetoes a bill?**

    A. It goes back to Congress which can override the veto with a two thirds vote

    B. It goes back to the Congressional committees

    C. It goes back to Congress which can override it with a three fourths vote

    D. It still becomes a law in any case

111. **The "Truman Doctrine" was an attempt to prevent the spread of:**

    A. German expansionism

    B. Imperialism

    C. Communism

    D. Fascism

112. **To impeach a president:**

    A. The charges are brought by the House of Representatives and tried in the Senate

    B. The charges are brought by the Senate and tried in the House of Representatives

    C. The charges are brought by the states and tried in Congress

    D. The charges are brought by Congress and tried before the Supreme Court

113. **In the United States the legal voting age is:**

    A. 19

    B. 18

    C. 21

    D. 25

114. **In the United States' electoral system who is allowed to vote in primary elections?**

   A. Generally, only registered party members are allowed to vote for their candidates in the party.

   B. Any registered voters may vote for candidates in either party primary

   C. Only voters actively engaged in party affairs may vote in a primary

   D. Generally, the United States does not engage in primary elections, though there are exceptions.

115. **A important *direct* consequence of the First World War was:**

   A. The end of European colonialism

   B. The Great Depression

   C. The rise of communism

   D. The end of fascism

116. **In journalism the term "muckraking" refers to:**

   A. An attempt to uncover alleged corruption of public officials

   B. The attempt to cover up the alleged corruption of public officials

   C. The process of buying up various media outlets

   D. The investigation of government inefficiency and waste

117. **The Voting Rights Act of 1965 sought to:**

   A. Extend the franchise to minorities

   B. Undo the last remaining features of unequal suffrage in the United States

   C. Establish the party primary

   D. Give the right to vote to women

118. The United States is a(n):

A. Direct democracy

B. Quasi-democracy

C. Semi-democracy

D. Indirect democracy

119. The United States is presently comprised of:

A. 52 states, the District of Columbia, and various overseas territories

B. 48 states, the District of Columbia, and various overseas territories

C. 50 states, the District of Columbia, and various overseas territories

D. 50 states and the District of Columbia only

120. Powers concurrent to both the federal and state governments are:

A. To tax, raise an army, to establish courts, to provide for the general welfare, and to fix the standards for weights and measures.

B. To tax, to charter banks, to borrow money, to make and enforce laws, and to provide for the general welfare.

C. To tax, to borrow money, to establish courts, to regulate international trade, and to make and enforce laws.

D. To ratify amendments, to tax, to make and enforce laws, to provide for the general welfare, and to raise a militia.

121. The term "Welfare Capitalism, or Welfare State", is used most often to describe:

   A. The former Soviet Union

   B. The interval between Mercantilism and Capitalism

   C. The United States and various European countries

   D. The Chinese experiments with Communism

122. A "Poll-Tax" is associated with:

   A. Tariffs on internationally traded goods

   B. Voting rights

   C. Government construction

   D. The income tax structure in a given state

123. Who of the following wrote about modern economic problems?

   A. John Locke

   B. Thomas Hobbes

   C. John Maynard Keynes

   D. Alexander Hamilton

124. "Gerrymandering" is:

   A. The consolidation of various voting districts into larger, more efficient entities

   B. The adjustment of voting districts in order to achieve some predetermined goal, usually to try to promote greater minority political representation.

   C. The removal of certain inefficient political departments

   D. The fixing of the economic infrastructure

125. The Spanish-American War broke out because of Spanish actions in:

   A. Florida

   B. Haiti

   C. Mexico

   D. Cuba

Answer Key

1. B	27. A	53. D	79. A	105. B
2. C	28. A	54. A	80. D	106. C
3. C	29. D	55. C	81. B	107. C
4. B	30. A	56. B	82. C	108. B
5. C	31. A	57. A	83. D	109. C
6. C	32. A	58. A	84. B	110. A
7. C	33. B	59. A	85. D	111. C
8. B	34. D	60. A	86. D	112. A
9. B	35. B	61. A	87. C	113. B
10. A	36. B	62. D	88. D	114. A
11. A	37. C	63. A	89. B	115. C
12. B	38. B	64. C	90. A	116. A
13. C	39. A	65. C	91. A	117. B
14. A	40. D	66. A	92. B	118. D
15. B	41. C	67. A	93. C	119. C
16. D	42. C	68. D	94. B	120. B
17. B	43. A	69. C	95. A	121. C
18. A	44. B	70. C	96. D	122. B
19. A	45. C	71. C	97. C	123. C
20. B	46. B	72. B	98. B	124. B
21. D	47. D	73. B	99. D	125. D
22. A	48. A	74. C	100. C	
23. C	49. A	75. D	101. C	
24. A	50. D	76. C	102. B	
25. B	51. C	77. C	103. D	
26. A	52. D	78. B	104. A	

Bibliography

For further reading, this guide contains the most up to date, and reliable information available to prepare for the exam. It has been specifically compiled to address the range of competencies and skills required on the exam. In addition, the following bibliography contains some additional basic reference sources that test candidates may use to prepare for the exam. These sources provide a framework for review of subject area knowledge to supplement this guide, textbooks, class work, and practical experience. The bibliography is based on those representative sources that committees of content consultants have recommended and are available in most college libraries and bookstores.

The Department of Education does not endorse any of these references as the only sources or references available that can be used for the exam. Many such comparable texts can be used, and the candidate is encouraged to explore a variety of reference sources.

1.   Armstrong, D. (1980) *Social Studies in Secondary Education.* New York: Macmillan

2.   Banks, J., & Clegg, A., Jr. (1985). *Teaching strategies for the social studies* (3rd ed.). New York: Longman.

3.   Dauer, M. (Ed). (1984). *Florida Politics and Government* (2nd ed.). Gainesville, FL. University of Florida Press.

4.   Gitelson, D. R., & Dubnick, M. (1988). *American Government.* Boston: Houghton Mifflin.

5.   Glassner, M., & deBlij, H. (1980). *Systematic Political Geography* (3rd ed.). New York: Wiley.

6.   Hagopian, M. (1978). *Regimes, Movements, and Ideologies: A Comparative Introduction to Political Science.* New York: Longman.

7.   Harris, F. (1986). *America's Democracy; The Ideal and the Reality* (3rd ed). Glenview, II. Scott, Foresman.

8.   Kelley,A. (1984). *Modem Florida Govemment.* Lanham, MA: University Press of America.

9.   Ladd, E. (1987). *The American Policy: The People and their Government* (2nd ed.). New York: Norton.

10.   Moffat, M., (1963). *Social Studies Instruction* (3rd) ed.). Unglued Cliffs N J.: Prentice-Hall.

11.   Morris, A., & Waldron, A. (1965). *Your Florida Government.* Gainesville, FL.: University of Florida Press.

12.   Morris, J. (Ed.). (1986). *Methods of Geographic Instruction.* Waltham, MA: Blaisdell.

13.   Rodee, C., Anderson, T., & Christol, C. (1967). *Introduction to Political Science* (2nd Ed.). New York: McGraw-Hill.

14.   Roe, B., Stodt, B., & Burns, P., (1987). *The Content Areas: Secondary School Reading Instruction* (3Rd Ed.). Boston: Houghton Mifflin.

15.   Roth, D., & Wilson, F., (1980). *The Comparative Study of Politics* (2nd ed.). Englewood Cliffs, NJ.: Prentice-Hall.

16.   U.S. Immigration and Naturalization Service. (1978). *Our Constitution and Government: Lessons on the Constitution and Government of the U.S. for use in the Public Schools by Candidates for Citizenship.* Washington, *DC: U.S.* Government Printing Office.

17.   Wilson, J., (1980). *American Government: Institutions and Policies.* Lexington, MA: Heath.